RECLAIMING WHAT WAS LOST

Carlyle Fielding Stewart, III

Recovering Spiritual
Vitality in the
Mainline Church

Abingdon Press
Nashville

RECLAIMING WHAT WAS LOST:
RECOVERING SPIRITUAL VITALITY IN THE MAINLINE CHURCH

Copyright © 2003 by Abingdon Press

This book is printed on acid-free paper.

Library of Congress Cataloging-in-Publication Data

Stewart, Carlyle Fielding, 1951-
    Reclaiming what was lost : recovering spiritual vitality in the mainline church / Carlyle Fielding Stewart, III.
        p. cm.
    Includes bibliographical references.
    ISBN 0-687-09787-8 (alk. paper)
    1. Church renewal. 2. Spirituality—United States. I. Title.

BV600.3.S74   2003
262'.001'7—dc21

2003002609

03 04 05 06 07 08 09 10 11 12—10 9 8 7 6 5 4 3 2 1
MANUFACTURED IN THE UNITED STATES OF AMERICA

To
The Reverend Dr. Elston Ricky Perry
The Reverend Dr. Delores Sconiers
The Reverend Vivian C. Bryant
Sojourners who are not ashamed to be
used by the Holy Ghost!

The church which is married to the Spirit of its Age will be a widow in the next.

—*Dean W. R. Inge*

Protestant: one who no longer protests.

—*Pete Skeris*

CONTENTS

ACKNOWLEDGMENTS

*Thanks to Yvette Nelson Williams,
my executive administrative assistant,
who typed portions of
manuscript revisions, and
the Reverend Vivian C. Bryant
for reviewing parts of it.*

INTRODUCTION

Mainline Protestantism is begging for spiritual renewal. Fortunately, such renewal is occurring in some sectors of mainline Protestantism, but in many sectors it is not. The old moorings of the past have given way to a new cynicism and atrophy that threatens the long-term health and viability of mainline churches. Some denominations are struggling to recapture the power of their past, but as many churches age and decline, they are threatened by a new obsolescence, and have regrettably lost touch with the present world. Speed Leas and George Parsons remind us, "The seeds of decline are found in our successes. . . . Our learned strengths have become our excesses" (*Understanding Your Congregation as a System*. Bethesda, Md.: Alban Institute, 1993, 1). Mainline Protestant churches must therefore find new ways of recovering spiritual vitality. The answer to revitalization can be found within many of the extant traditions of those churches.

Effective models of church growth and empowerment require leaders to possess the courage to conceptualize and implement new paradigms of ministry in the local church. If the church is to positively grow and reach more persons for Christ, pastoral and laity leaders must establish a clear vision and purpose of the church and its ministries. They must return to basics and open themselves to the power of spiritual transformation. Thus the structure and mission of the church are not simply shaped by theoretical *texts* that define and limit the church within traditional parameters, but are also influenced by the practical *contexts, communities,* and *cultures* that create environments in which those ministries are innovatively conceived, developed, and actualized. They are also influenced by the climate of spiritual development in those churches.

Frequently, models of ministry and church leadership are cultivated through theoretical or textbook methodologies that can be informative and helpful, but are not fitted to peculiar contexts of ministry. Pastors and laity all have ideas of what ministry should constitute in the broadest sense of the term, but the means and assumptions of ministry must also be influenced by the communities and experiences of the people they serve. Positive ministry is based upon information that is both theoretical and empirical, formal and practical. Positive ministry is also influenced by the spiritual climate of mainline churches.

Hence it makes little sense to simply adopt a theoretically preconceived model of ministry for a particular congregation without adapting it to the environment and ethos, the community and culture of the people within that specific context. Leadership that is both relevant and positively growth oriented will cultivate and employ both textual and contextual approaches to ministry that will in turn empower local churches to reach more people for Christ. Gone are the days when pastors and laity could simply grab a model of ministry, and imperically impose it upon a particular culture and people because it is denominationally correct, and expect lucrative, long-term results.

One recurring struggle in mainline denominations in general is the development of a hegemonic culture of thinking, which confines the way we conceive ministry and minister and restricts the creative implementation of new ideas and fresh leadership paradigms. This problem is particularly acute in denominations, where, in an effort to develop min-

14

istries according to the texts and culture of the denomination (every denomination has its own assumptive culture for ministry), the development obviates the cultural and spiritual needs of the people in the community and thus often fails to win them to Christ. The failure to cultivate cultural relevancy, along with the absence of a genuine Christ-centered spiritual vitality, often leads to the demise of many churches.

Too often ethnic congregations within these denominations have adopted *assimilative models of ministry* which appropriate Anglo-American culture while negating the positive aspects of their own culture as viable pretexts for ministry. However, the affirmation and celebration of one's own culture is indispensable to growing churches. This is particularly true in black churches. The lamentable result is a modicum of strong, vibrant black churches within predominantly white, mainline, Protestant denominations that exude the Holy Spirit and have creative and culturally relevant ministries. The fact that black churches are being closed in urban areas throughout the U.S. exemplifies the broader and local church's failure to develop meaningful and innovative ministries that speak to the real needs of the African American masses.

To unilaterally appropriate models of ministry from the larger culture and arbitrarily impose them on the African American community simply because it is "theologically correct" is highly problematic. Doing this without regard to the psycho-spiritual-cultural needs of, in this case, black people equally compounds the problem. A more plausible approach would be to design ministries and leadership modalities that speak to the needs and cultures of specific communities in ways that will both empower and nurture the churches and communities they serve.

Too often models of ministry that are more culturally specific to the needs of certain communities and not to the culture of mainline denominations are viewed as an anomaly. Thus, cultural variety can lead in some quarters of the church to a form of denominational delegitimization. This thinking is problematic because it assumes that although the denomination has a history, polity, and doctrine that have shaped its own models and understandings of ministry, it also contends that culturally and contextually such ministries should all be homogeneous. In an effort to preserve a uniform structure of church governance and life, and to vouchsafe its unique heritage, some believe that ministry should be a monolithic, unilateral configuration. This belief negates the cultural multiplicities and variances that constitute the diversity of the church's constituencies and undermines its true strengths as a denomination. The assumption here is that because all members within a denomination have a unified theological framework for ministry, share a common history, doctrine and polity, that such ecclesiastical and theological uniformity will translate into ministries that that will be identical in every cultural context.

This assertion has been a major stumbling block in particular for African American Methodism, because it denies cultural diversity and virtually repudiates culturally creative approaches to ministry as summarily non-United Methodist. However, the great genius of United Methodism is the way it has allowed for the various expressions of culture, not in the way it has assimilated or homogenized cultural opposition.

For example, again, a major problem for black United Methodist churches is the manner in which they have unilaterally appropriated the culture of United Methodism without adapting it to the cultural and spiritual needs of African American communities. Many church leaders, both white and black, have yet to learn that black people do not join churches because of the name or polity of a denomination. Instead, they join a church because of its culture, its styles of ministry and worship, and because it meets some deeper spiritual and psychological need that speaks to issues of identity, empowerment, and spiritual transformation.

For example, one black pastor had difficulty developing a rites of passage program for youth in his community because it was not mandated by his church's denominational *Discipline.* Instead of establishing the program based upon *contextual needs*—that is to say, because wayward youth in his community needed such a mentoring program—he rejected the idea because it didn't fit the *texts* of the church's rule book. Thus, a viable program which could have evolved from contextual need was discarded because it wasn't prescribed as a legitimate course of action in the church's *Discipline.* This pastor failed to understand that the rule book did not preclude his developing a rites of passage program. Needed here was some contextual common sense and the courage to develop ministries based on the real needs of his constituencies. He did not realize that he did not need permission from his superiors to develop viable ministries which would empower his community and subsequently help his church grow. Developing a rites of passage program based on contextual needs could have given his church an opportunity to witness and empower youths. The real need of mentoring youths could have necessitated the implementation of the program. This pastor failed to recognize that people largely never joined his church because of denomination, but because it had pertinent programs that had met their needs. In this case, his ideas of what was denominationally appropriate impeded an opportunity for church growth.

A similar problem can be viewed in the praxis of spirituality. Scholar Monroe Forham reminds us that religion meets the adaptive and expressive needs of a community. Although many mainline churches largely gained power by their capacity to meet the expressive needs of their communities, as they become more formal and institutionalized, meeting those needs seems to have become less of a concern. It appears that as the larger culture has become more outwardly expressive, mainline churches have become more reticent. As mainline churches have become more hierarchical, institutional, and formally structured, the concern seems to be more with preserving the institutions. Thus the spiritual vitality of local congregations is measured more in terms of how well those churches conform to institutional protocol than in how well they save souls and transform lives in their local contexts. Being loyal to the larger church means preserving and perpetuating the institutional hierarchy (each church paying its apportionments, giving service to the conference, etc.). The aim should not be to preserve the institutional hierarchy and *then* save souls. The first priority should be saving souls and then the hierarchy is inherently preserved. Perhaps a "both and" rather than an "either or" approach could be developed.

Given these types of problems, the reconfiguration and establishment of new leadership paradigms warrant a serious analysis of the texts, contexts, and the way we understand and practice our spiritual foundations of ministry. Not only must we consider the theoretical frameworks for the practice of ministry, but also the praxis cultures and spirituality of specific communities. The cultural and contextual assumptions for ministry in Anglo-American communities may be highly differentiated, slightly differentiated, or similar to those in African American and other communities. This is not a negative assessment. It simply means that people have varying assumptions, understandings, and perceptions about what is meaningful, viable, and relevant as they seek to have a genuine experience of God. These different assumptions often translate into different religious and spiritual modalities that are based on the adaptive and expressive needs of the people.

A new church leadership paradigm must therefore consider the cultivation of ministries that are based on the psycho-socio-spiritual-cultural needs of specific communities. The task is to develop models of ministry that embrace, transcend, and transform so that the missional objectives of both church and community have a unified, transformative framework. Reconfiguring new leadership paradigms means that pastors and laity take seriously the means by which the texts of ministry shape the context, and the context of ministry shapes the texts. Mainline churches have done both these things in the past and there is no reason why they cannot do this in the future. For spiritual revitalization to occur, mainline churches must go back to the basics by emphasizing models of spirituality that meet the practical and social needs of people and by developing styles and modes of ministry that are both contextually and culturally relevant.

Reclaiming What Was Lost highlights eleven basic principles or steps that will strengthen and reclaim God's church. These steps have been developed as a result of my traveling and helping various churches throughout the country to develop paradigms and models for church growth that will meet the needs of the people they are called to serve.

1

RECLAIMING CHRIST THROUGH A CONVERSION OR RECONVERSION EXPERIENCE

I went to America to convert the Indians, but oh! who shall convert me?
—John Wesley

If the mainline church is going to reclaim and strengthen God's church, then it must adopt a plan for spiritual wellness and vitality. Writer Thomas Bandy tells us that churches must learn to kick addictive habits if they are to thrive and grow. Healthy churches are essential for long-term growth and empowerment. My contention is that spirituality and spiritual vitality are important hallmarks of healthy congregations and healthy leaders. The undergirding, underlying basis of all numerical growth in the church is spiritual growth. If churches are to survive and succeed in the future as they have in the past, they must adopt plans for spiritual revitalization, spiritual wellness, and renewal as part of their spiritual mantra for the future.

21

Furthermore, the current malaise and atrophy churches have experienced throughout this nation are largely due to spiritual "dis-ease," bad habits, and problems that have compelled the church away from its fundamental mission. Major denominations, like United Methodism, have lost and continue to lose members annually. The principles contained in *Reclaiming What Was Lost*, then, are meant for these churches and their leaders. What then can be done to empower the church and its leaders for the future?

The first step is to reclaim Christ through a conversion or reconversion experience. There is an underlying assumption that every person in the church has had a conversion experience, has been born again, or has a saving relationship with Jesus Christ. What I have seen and experienced in my travels throughout United Methodism and other denominations is the practice of organized religion (organized, systematic *ecclesia*—a Greek term used in the New Testament for *church*) that is often confused with the practice of Christian spirituality. Many people practice an organized religion, or the culture of a specific congregation, more than they practice Christ. Practicing Christ is a disciplined devotion. It means developing the spiritual will and commitment that will empower believers in their daily walk with God on earth. I can go to church religiously but if I have not, after all my years of church attendance, developed a basic practical spirituality that can be applied in my daily life, I am still without the foundation that makes me strong spiritually. The practice of Christian spirituality presupposes a daily dialogical relationship with Christ. If I am in spiritual relationship with Christ intimately, I will ultimately reference and index Christ as a source of power and strength in my daily walk with him. All of this points to a genuine conversion experience in which Christ becomes the ultimate guide, source, and transformative and informative resource for daily living.

There are many leaders in church who have been given the task of leading God's people, who have never had a conversion experience, know nothing about being born again, and largely do not have a personal dialogical relationship with Christ. How can the church go, grow, and glow if the leaders have not claimed Christ as the center and anchor of their lives? How can Christians effectively lead God's people God's way if they have not yet been convicted or convinced of God's transforming love and grace?

Reclaiming Christ means that the church and its leadership take seriously the ministry, mind, spirit, and mandates of Christ as a foundation for kingdom building. Leaders need to be converted or reconverted to Christ, and both mainline denominations and their local churches need a conversion experience so that the practice of true, Christian spirituality will inform and direct the practice of organized *ecclesia*. The church is the only institution that preserves the gospel and should be a vehicle by which and through which the gospel is proclaimed, disseminated, and practiced. Unfortunately, everyone in the church is not in Christ and Christ is not in them. What happened to saving souls and conversion experience? Why do we no longer talk about salvation and offer it both to the people who come inside and to those outside of the church's four walls? What happened to those basic practices that gave us spiritual strength and vitality? Conversion is a very important part of Christian spirituality. Conversion should occur in our thinking and in our willingness to be used by Christ for the transformation of ourselves and the world.

CONVERTING THE CHURCH TO CHRIST

In order for the church to be reenergized, it must also have a conversion or reconversion experience. Individuals need genuine conversion, and then the church at large can experience redemption and salvation.

The church needs a conversion experience from the constraints of institutionalism and organized religion to the practice of wholesome, vital, energized Christian spirituality.

This means prescribing the things that empower people spiritually such as: bringing their Bibles to church, reading their Bibles, engaging in Bible study, developing a devotional life, and learning how to pray. It also involves the daily, disciplined practice of Christian spirituality. It means developing the will to organize one's life so that the practice of spirituality becomes part of one's daily routine. This is true spiritual power. Developing a habit of daily devotion not only allows the believer to have an intentional encounter with God, but also each act of devotion is inherently an act of submission—an act of acknowledgment that Jesus is Lord. Every time a believer engages in the devotional act, he or she is acknowledging and affirming that God is the ultimate source and reason for his or her existence. Devotion and praise accord to God the reverence and adulation that God so deeply deserves. We are powerless if our faith is not rooted in a practical spirituality of devotion. These are the imperatives of developing the discipline of daily devotion.

This also means converting those tiring structures that sap our energy and zap our drive from being bastions of positive vitality and growth. Our institutional life and its varying demands often routinize, mechanize, and anesthetize us to the need for reconversion. Are we doing church work or the work of the church? Many are caught in the labyrinths and mazes of meetings and more meetings. We do need committees. We do need structures. However, God so loved the world that he didn't send a committee. Moreover, a camel is a horse planned by a committee that is composed of the unfit in league with the unqualified who draft the unwilling to do the unnecessary. We need committees and structures but they often wear us down and steal our vim and vigor. We need fresh watering places to restore our souls, and church meetings often will not do it. Too often committees become ends within themselves rather than vehicles of grace for Christ's transforming power.

Christ was a spiritual energizer. He left his carpenter's trade and galvanized the disciples for ministry. His work was the ministry of hope, empowerment, and positive transformation. He touched, healed, and converted people. Remember the man who was healed and went away from Jesus jumping, and kicking because he had received new life? Conversions give new life and energy to the converted. Jesus changed this man's understanding of who he was and who God is. This man's understanding of himself was changed and converted into something positive and beautiful and it would have a lasting influence on the rest of his life.

In my travels around the country, I frequently encounter people who have never had a conversion experience, people in leadership positions who have no devotional life, never read their Bibles, never tithe, and who are not in spiritual formation. They have little zeal, energy, or passion for God's work. People join churches because their parents were members, their friends are members, or because it is convenient, but they never have had a conversion experience, never come to know Jesus Christ personally in vital relationship with him as their Lord and Savior. They never move beyond an opinion of God to a genuine, dialogical relationship with God. Too many of us are simply Christians in name only. We don't know Christ personally so we can't serve him loyally. We are simply going through church motions. We have been in the church all of our lives and never develop a genuine saving, loving, redeeming relationship with Jesus Christ. We are still living between good Friday and Easter morning. We never obtain the resurrection spirit or power that Christ grants us as his people. We have not been renewed or re-energized for service.

The church needs to be converted to Christ, while nominal, perfunctory Christians need a reconversion experience. Some people have just enough religion to make them miserable. These people have not truly been converted. They do not have a hunger for God's Word and they are basically lost. Yet these people set the agenda for God's church. The people with limited vision usually attempt to dictate the agenda for

25

people who have unlimited vision in Christ. They are in positions of authority and power. They are entrusted with making important decisions about the church's future but are not rooted spiritually and grounded relationally in Christ. Their qualification for service is based more on secular than spiritual criteria. They are the "blind leading the blind." Many people confess their ignorance and know that they do not know God and will seek a remedy for it. Others are content to not be converted and believe that they are perfectly correct in their thinking. How can I become an effective witness for Christ when I do not know him, if I have not been converted by or to him?

How can people be converted to Christ when we, as instruments, have not been converted, reconverted, convicted, or convinced that he lives? How can we serve as instruments of conversion when we have not experienced God's "Amazing Grace" and "Blessed Assurance"? How are we to revitalize the church through Christ when our preaching lacks verve and verse, preparation and imagination, where our singing is tired and our serving is elegiac and anemic? Have the ministers and laity in your church had a conversion experience? Is it business as usual or business unusual, or has conversion gone out of style? We must stress the value of conversion.

Conversion is a hallmark of spiritual vitality and growing churches. Converts are not ashamed of the gospel. They are not ashamed of being Christian. They are not wary or shy about the God who has brought them, kept them, and saved them. Those touched by Christ have a joy, a power, a spirit that cannot be quenched or muted by the routines and conventions of church life.

We need to emphasize first time conversion and reconversion for those cloyed and numbed by the routines and demands of organized, institutional *ecclesia*. Conversion brings hope, renewal, energy, and vitality and we must find ways of sustaining such ardor in the life of the church. Does your church need to be converted to Christ, converted from the labyrinth of the institutional church to the praxis of vital Christian spirituality?

Denominational officials, clergy, and laity must find ways to challenge their churches to emphasize the importance of conversion. Conversion begins with the self. Most denominational theologies include conversion as a vital element in Christian faith and practice. The problem is in the practice of theology within the local church; many local congregations have placed more emphasis on survival and keeping the doors open or maintaining homeostasis than on converting souls to Christ. Leaders of various mainline churches must find ways of revaluing the dynamics of spiritual conversion. Too frequently burdened by the cares and demands of the church's institutional life, denominational officers have themselves lost sight of the importance of conversion and being born anew in Christ. Needed today is a fresh anointing of the Holy Spirit—a new power and vitality that is rooted in Christ.

Perhaps church officials should relegate the operation of their institutions to professional management companies so they can go about the true business of reaching and touching more souls for Christ. Rather than being inundated and preoccupied with serving the church hierarchy and tending to its bureaucratic and operational machinery, the main of such work can be given to companies that specialize in tending to institutional structures, so that church officials can get about the business of revitalizing and converting their constituencies for Christ, and of revamping their organizational structures. Before true conversion can be experienced, the thinking and orientation of denominational officials, as well as clergy and laity, must be radically transformed. Denominational officials must be challenged to think outside the box.

SUMMARY

Have you had a conversion experience with or to Christ? Have you ever had your heart "strangely warmed" or experienced the power of the Holy Spirit "like fire shut up in my bones"? Before we can preach, teach, and witness with spiritual power and authority we need a conversion experience. If mainline churches are to experience spiritual revitalization, the importance and necessity of spiritual conversion must be emphasized.

2

RECLAIMING THE BIBLE AS AN UNDERGIRDING AUTHORITY FOR MINISTRY

Nobody ever outgrows Scripture; the book widens and deepens with our years. —*Charles Haddon Spurgeon*

To recover spiritual vitality, the church must reclaim the Bible and Word centeredness as the central undergirding authorities for ministry. This may sound highly basic, mundane, rudimentary, and fundamental and this is precisely the point. We must return to the basics that won us success in the early days. Reading our Bibles, bringing our Bibles to church, and attending Bible study are important steps in banning the scriptural illiteracy that is killing our churches.

In a time when the Bible is available in so many versions and languages, how is it that it remains the least read book for so many Christians? There are men's, women's, and family devotional Bibles, and Bibles in almost every language.

How then can the church have viable leaders who never attend Bible study, bring their Bibles to church, or read their Bibles for devotion? In fact, the only time they seem to open their Bibles is when they pull them from the pew when the Scripture is read on Sunday morning. Many people in our modern culture have problems reading anything longer than a paragraph, let alone a Bible. In fact, before many people determine whether something is worth reading, they will first determine its length and the time it will take to read it. Our lives are filled with so many other trivial pursuits that Bible reading or Bible study is almost an anomaly. Any Christian who is serious in seeking Christ must view the Bible as an invaluable resource for spiritual growth and empowerment. Christians must revalue the purpose and power of Scripture. They must be willing to use the Bible as a resource for enhancing their awareness and understanding of God. The Bible must be seen as user-friendly, easy to read, and empowering in every aspect of the believer's life. If the church is to truly reclaim spiritual power, the current aversions to reading and using the Bible as an undergirding source for ministry must end. In the Word of God there's power, information, and instruction that will help the believer grow in his or her awareness of Christ.

THE NEED FOR WORD CENTEREDNESS AND SCRIPTURAL LITERACY

Scriptural illiteracy is killing our churches. What is the difference between the person who can't read his Bible and the person who can read but never reads his Bible? The man who can read is also illiterate in the sense of being ignorant of God's Word. We must develop the will to overcome those obstacles and constraints preventing us from reading and studying our Bibles regularly. Too many things in our daily lives keep us from seeking God and studying God's Word.

The Bible should be valued, affirmed, and explored as a source of power, joy, and strength for those seeking God. Scriptural literacy does not mean having the ability to readily quote Bible verses to impress others or to show off how religious and righteous we are. Instead it is an intentional, sustained, and systematic examination of the Word of God as part of the spiritual formation and life of any congregation so that the Word may take root in us.

Unfortunately, there are too many church leaders who don't read their Bibles, don't reference Scripture in their work with God's people, don't attend Bible study, nor are they in any type of spiritual formation or development. We have failed to set a spiritual criteria for those who lead in God's church. We have failed to stress the importance of Bible literacy and spiritual formation as foundations for leadership in God's church. I have been in numerous situations where leaders conducted church meetings without devotional time or referencing Scripture as an undergirding strength for their work. Many leaders are ignorant of the Word and have no desire to discover its power and value. They lead, make decisions, conduct church business, and influence people without ever having read or referenced God's Holy Word. How can leaders spiritually lead others in God's work if they are oblivious to God's Word? This is one of the great tragedies and dilemmas of the modern church—leaders who are scripturally and spiritually illiterate and who undercut their spiritual power by their ignorance and underutilization of the Bible. It is small wonder that so many churches flounder in their service for Christ.

Illiteracy involves not knowing the Bible and refusing to want to know it or use it as a basis for interpreting the church's purpose and mission to the world. How can leaders lead in the faith community as the Body of Christ when they have no understanding of what the Word requires and demands of them as they serve God's people and call God's people back to God?

31

Scriptural literacy is indispensable to giving viable spiritual leadership in the church. Knowledge of Scripture will also help leaders to grow in their awareness of God and enable them to resolve conflict spiritually and biblically, most often leading to reconciliation and wholeness among dislocated believers. We must go back to our denominational basics of Bible study and reading, of developing a devotional life, and of cultivating a life that is rooted in prayer and spiritual disciplines as foundations for nurturing God's church and building God's kingdom. Bible literacy must become a requirement for all leaders in God's church.

BACK TO BASSICS

In addition to Bible literacy, we must get back to the basics of *cultivating spiritual gifts and spiritual fruit, healing*, and *service*. Why is there so much resistance regarding word centeredness, leadership under the guidance and direction of the Holy Ghost or Holy Spirit?

One reason may be that as education levels have risen, people have incorrectly assumed that this suffices for biblical knowledge and understanding. How can we grow as a church when people are ignorant of the Word of God? How can people develop strong, robust spiritual lives when they are only fed spiritual food once a week through preaching? Many people are starving to death spiritually because they are undernourished. A spiritually undernourished church is a spiritually unhealthy church and a spiritually unhealthy church will eventually end up dead on arrival or on life support. Preaching, teaching, reaching, and serving should be biblically based.

The importance of developing biblical hermeneutics is equally valuable. Valuing the Bible also means teaching it according to various hermeneutical precepts and principles. Leaders and believers should not only read their Bibles daily, but develop strong and accurate interpretive skills. Readers should know the difference between literal and figurative interpretation, discern between microscopic and telescopic modes of analysis, and develop some familiarity of the difference between exegesis and isogesis.

Reclaiming the Bible for spiritual power also suggests that we develop methods of responsible analysis and interpretation that will be true to both the text and context of scriptural passages.

SUMMARY

We need to go back to basics in our church: planting and growing. We should dispel Bible illiteracy, spiritual ignorance, and other realities that have contributed to our decline. We must delve into our past and find elements of the work of early church leaders that give us power, purpose, and presence in the communities we serve.

The Bible remains one of our most important resources and must be unequivocally reclaimed as an undergirding authority in ministry if churches are to have true biblical and spiritual power. Mainline Protestantism cannot experience spiritual revitalization without valuing and revering the Bible as a primary resource for spiritual growth, development, and empowerment. By emphasizing the need for Bible basics, mainline churches can teach and train a whole new generation of disciples.

3

RECLAIMING THE TRADITION OF HOLINESS

A true love of God must begin with delight in his holiness, and not delight in any other attribute, for no other attribute is truly lovely without this.

–Jonathan Edwards, A Treatise Concerning Religious Affections

We must reclaim a tradition of holiness. What happened to holiness? Nothing seems to be sacred anymore. There is a certain energy and power that issues from holiness and sanctification. Holiness has its own energy, trajectory, powers, and capacities. Holiness and sanctification provide the believer with a spiritual power that can sustain hope and belief under conditions of hopelessness, apostasy, and unbelief. Why do the prospects of holy living frighten the "hell" out of some of us? Holiness means being set aside and consecrated for service and life. Why all the disdain and contempt for holy living today?

I have met many people in my journey whom I love,

admire, and respect who are holy people. Although they are not ashamed of being holy nor are they invasive with it, they have often been made to feel like spiritual freaks. They have been ostracized, ridiculed, and often rebuked as people who think they are better than everyone else. The tragedy is they are often repudiated by other so-called Christians within the church. Why are some people, leaders, and churches afraid to reference and invoke or discuss the power and workings of the Holy Ghost? Why are people uncomfortable talking about the Holy Spirit or Holy Ghost, or developing a language or lexicon of holiness? Now I don't mean here "holier-than-thou-ness" or "I-am-better-than-you-ness," this game Christians often play that alienates and repels rather than welcomes and attracts others to Christ. What I mean is living holy, sanctified lives.

In our effort to be all things to all people, have we accommodated the secular culture and allowed popular culture and the larger society to douse the fires of holiness and spirituality? Sanctification, saving souls, offering salvation, walking the talk are important hallmarks of the church leaders. Do leaders have a saving relationship with Jesus Christ? Are they living the word? Do the word and Holy Spirit dwell within them?

We must reclaim our tradition of holiness and be open to the outpouring and anointing of the Holy Ghost in our ministries. We should invoke and reference the Holy Spirit as a guide and index for all that we do in ministry.

OUR TRADITION OF HOLINESS

We must begin by understanding that as an institutional church, we have lost some of our focus and vitality. Our focus at times is too horizontal rather than vertical. We need to get spiritually vertical. We stress the importance of working in community, building community, and tending to organizational structures but often forget to invoke the presence and power of the Holy Spirit as a foundation and guide for what we do. We need the horizontal and vertical focus that is our cross. We are torn between horizontal needs and our vertical calling as people of God. Our focus should then be outward and upward. For example, ministers of the gospel serve God's people horizontally in community through their position as pastor. However, they are called by God vertically to serve them through the practice of spirituality.

We must reclaim a tradition of holiness, where we invoke the presence and power of the Holy Ghost or Holy Spirit into the direction and leadership of the church. What happened to holiness? Holiness, which emphasizes our horizontal responsibility to the communities we serve and the vertical anointing of God for service? Sometimes our focus is so horizontally oriented that we leave God out of the affairs of the church. Holiness means consecration and being set aside for doing God's work, while holier-than-thou-ness subordinates and humiliates people under a hierarchy of pseudospiritual authority.

What happened to the language and traditions of holiness in our churches? Why are people uncomfortable referencing the Holy Ghost, and invoking the Holy Spirit into the life and affairs of the church? Why do we not talk of holiness, saving souls, and converting people to Christ? Why do we appear to have distanced ourselves from such conversation? Why are some of us ashamed or embarrassed by talking of the need for holiness in the church? Do we believe that holiness for Christ is no longer in style, vogue, or has credence and power? What happened to the fires that come with holiness? Does holiness, for some, mean not being in control of oneself for service? Are we afraid of being holy?

Again, this is not holier-than-thou-ness, where we agitate, badger, and antagonize others in the name of Christ. Instead this is about a vitality, an energy, a spirit, a dexterity, a resiliency, a confidence, and a determination that exudes assurance, conviction, sincerity, sanctity, liberty, and love for God's people and God's church.

Part of our lethargy stems from our unwillingness to look upwardly, outwardly, and inwardly to God and to genuinely invoke and petition God's anointive power and the traditions of holiness as guideposts for developing our churches. We have become arrogantly narcissistic and myopic as we look only to ourselves for answers and leave God out of the power and the process. One writer said the problem is not denying the existence of God but living as though God did not exist. Does the church sometimes conduct itself as though the people, and not God, are solely responsible for its purpose and destiny?

At what point do we ask God to truly lead, guide, and direct us in kingdom building? At what juncture do we empty ourselves of self-absorption and invoke the Holy Spirit as a catalyst for our decision making in the church? How do we contextualize ourselves into the movement of the spirit so that the Holy Spirit leads, anoints, directs, and empowers the ministry of Christ? Seldom do people talk about holiness, saving souls, or being converted to Christ anymore. It's almost as if such talk is too evangelical, too foundational, too fundamental for our middle-class, erudite, secular, and educated sensibilities. Have we moved so far away from the foundations of our spiritual traditions that we have lost our identity as a church? These are our foundations. These are the cornerstones of God's work. How can we omit the reality of holiness and the power that comes with it? Holiness was an integral element in the flourishing of many mainline denominations.

When we talk of reclaiming a tradition of holiness, we mean developing a spiritual holiness that will culminate into social holiness for transformation and empowerment of God's people on the personal and social levels. Too often the practice of organized, institutional *ecclesia*, routinized religion impedes and eclipses the need for holiness practice as a foundation for church growth and empowerment. Holiness should also compel the transformation of the injustices of society. The awareness that comes with holiness compels transformative witness on behalf of the poor and oppressed. Those who are holy have an eye and a feel for the spirit of God. They have a joy that comes from knowing, walking with, and serving God and the people. Holy people exude a certain air of confidence and humility, determination, and destiny in their walk with God. They possess something vital and special, something lasting and loving that adds value to themselves and to the people they know and serve. Holiness means adding spiritual value—divine power—to people, places, and things of this world. It means sharing the light of Christ in ways that illuminate Christ's power and presence in a world wallowing in darkness. Some people are not afraid to be set aside, to shine their light for Christ. Bold and creative, they are unfazed by the power and trappings of this world. They live in love and they speak truth. Their interests are serving God and living in God's spirit. They concur wholly with Galatians 1:10, "Am I now trying to win the approval of men, or of God? . . . If I were still trying to please men, I would not be a servant of Christ" (NIV).

People who are holy have an aura about them that speaks of the majesty and mystery of Christ. What then distinguishes the church from the world, the secular from the sacred, the sacred from the profane? If we have not holiness, then what distinguishes us from others? What is the badge of our identity as Christians? What is our calling card? Too often the church seeks to fit in with the world by saying, "We are just like you." The implication here is that because we are just like you we are no better than you. By what, then, can we claim spiritual authority if the church is just like the world? If the church is no different from the world, why should the world be converted to Christ? The world would, it seems, be much better off just by staying and being itself.

Holiness is the mark of distinction: an element that distinguishes the church and Christ from the world. If the church has no sense of the holy, no sense of the sacred, then how can it truly do the work of Christ in the world? The church needs to stop trying to imitate the world and put on the mind, spirit, and holiness of Christ. The church needs to stop apologizing to the world for wanting to be holy and Christlike. Leaders and laity in the church need to stop hiding their holiness behind closed doors and by taking refuge in the darkened corridors of this world. Christ calls us to be holy,s to be full of the divine light and love that he gives us. We as the church should reclaim holiness and unapologetically share its gifts with a dying world.

SUMMARY

We become holy when we relinquish our lives to Christ by walking in his light and by embodying and sharing his love. We become holy by opening ourselves truly and fully to the Holy Spirit. We become holy by the disciplined practice of prayer, Bible study, and Christian service. We become holy by turning on and leaving on the light of Christ within us. We are holy when we translate the power, energy, and vitality of the divine spirit into making the society and the world a better place.

Holiness should be our hallmark and benchmark. We should recognize, affirm, and welcome the gifts and fruits of the Holy Spirit. Mainline Protestantism should unabashedly reclaim holiness as a spiritual goal of all Christian striving. Holiness means setting apart for divine purposes. This should be an overriding concern if churches are to become healthy and vital for the present age. Without holiness, the church loses sanctity, direction, and Holy Ghost power in facing the challenges of the present and future.

4

RECLAIMING THE LEGITIMACY OF ALL SPIRITUAL GIFTS

A spiritual gift is a God-given ability to serve God and other Christians in such a way that Christ is glorified and believers are edified.   —*Warren Wiersbe*

A talent becomes a spiritual gift when we use it in service of God. **We must reclaim the legitimacy of all spiritual gifts by cultivating an ethos of gifting in the church.** How did we get to the point where only certain types of spiritual gifts became acceptable gifts in our practice of ministry? In looking at many mainline Protestant denominations, why are only certain types of gifts stressed as opposed to the other more charismatic gifts? What happened to the gifts of tongues and the interpretation of tongues, the gifts of wisdom, discernment, and healing?

If the church is truly the church, should it not cultivate an atmosphere where *all* gifts are welcomed and nurtured and not just those that we consider tame, sane, or acceptable? If the Holy Ghost is truly at work in our church, should we not

41

have a manifestation of all gifts? Spiritual gifts lead to the manifestation of spiritual fruit. Are we playing God when we say that we will only allow certain types of gifts and all others are not allowed? Is God pleased with this? Is God truly at work here? Do we choke off the Holy Spirit's power to manifest other spiritual gifts by our own prejudices and predilections? As I have visited various mainline churches, I seldom if ever see the manifestation of the more charismatic or prophetic gifts of the Holy Spirit. Why? Have we become more concerned about controlling and managing the affairs of the church to the point of stifling the emergence of other spiritual gifts? Are too many churches more concerned about domesticating the spirit, establishing order and decorum by reinforcing certain polite forms of behavior than allowing the Holy Spirit to come in and have its way in the church and in our hearts? We want controlled worship, controlled order, controlled service, controlled everything. Who are we to dictate to God and the Holy Spirit what gifts will be manifested and expressed in the life of the church? One of the reasons some mainline churches have died and others are dying a slow agonizing death is due to the advertent and inadvertent suppression of all the gifts of the Holy Spirit. When we try to control every outcome and to create a climate where all gifts cannot potentially flourish, we diminish our divine possibilities for bearing spiritual fruit.

Because many of these churches are more interested in maintaining order and discipline than in allowing a sovereign Holy Spirit to order their steps, many churches have become underdeveloped or stagnated in their growth both spiritually and numerically. The Holy Spirit anoints and grants spiritual gifts. When churches say we want only certain types of gifts versus other type of gifts, they are writing off the full power of the Holy Spirit's capacity to produce spiritual fruit in all aspects of the church's ministry.

Too many churches seem more interested in maintaining their "chill status" than being turned on to the penetrating, de-icing fires of the Holy Ghost. Does God call us to simply chill, control, and have dominion over the church? The church should welcome and open itself to the full presence of all spiritual gifts. It is true that not all churches will manifest all spiritual gifts, but some churches have created a deadly climate of repression that does not allow certain types of gifts to flourish. Spiritual gifts are like other things in life that grow. They need the proper "son light," nourishment, cultivation, and water. Without these things they will not take root, germinate, and blossom. When we "pick and choose" the types of spiritual gifts we prefer having, rather than allowing the Holy Spirit to deploy to us freely the gifts we need to grow, we are saying to God that you are really not wanted or needed here except where and how we tell you.

Many mainline churches have stymied the ability of the Holy Spirit to manifest other spiritual gifts that will keep those churches alive, vital, and open to God. By not fostering an environment or creating a milieu where all spiritual gifts are welcome, churches have limited their capacity to grow and glow as God would have them.

Some churches never discuss, explore, or cultivate an ethos of gifting. They have created church cultures that choke off the life of the spirit and stagnate the emergence of spiritual gifts. If God is to reclaim the church, we must cultivate an environment in which all spiritual gifts can flourish.

Each church should do a spiritual gifts inventory with parishioners in order to help people discover, cultivate, and match their gifts with various ministries. People have a need for ministry areas that meet their passions and create a context for their gifts to be actualized. As a congregation, ask:

- Do we discourage the use of spiritual gifts?

- Do we find only certain gifts acceptable?

- Are we creating a climate where new gifts cannot grow or flourish?

- What is the ethos of gifting in our church?

- Are people encouraged to use their gifts unashamedly and without apology, or are their gifts suppressed?

When we create a climate for gifting, we create a context for reenergizing and renewing God's church according to God's infinite possibilities. When we suppress and restrict people's gifts, we cut off their potential to spiritually grow and empower God's ministry God's way. When a farmer was asked the reasons for such a healthy annual crop, his reply was, "I am never cheap with the seed." The more you plant the more you grow. And so it is with the church. The more we plant the seeds for spiritual gifts to grow the more fruit we bear in ministry.

A minister remarked upon his retirement that he had met two types of people in the church: *trees* and *posts*. Planted trees grow and bear fruit. Planted posts wither and die. No amount of nurturing will cause a post to grow. But the right type of nurturing and cultivation will cause the tree to grow. Spiritual gifts are like trees that need planting and nurturing to grow and, if done correctly, the ministry can bear much fruit.

We must remember that we cannot simply have a management mentality in the church. Maintaining what is and controlling what will be, while helpful, also hurts spiritual vitality. We cannot manage ourselves into the future or manage ourselves into future prosperity. Management, by nature, creates a certain type of energy that maintains something rather than grows something. Managing and growing are two different types of energy. Booker T. Washington observed that there were two ways of exerting strength: one is by pushing down and the other is by pulling up. When we simply manage or maintain, we create an environment that often is directed toward keeping things in their place rather than pushing things beyond their limit to actualize their potential.

Craig Hickman said we need people who have the minds of managers but the souls of leaders. We need people who can analyze and manage institutions, but people who can envision, enliven, and encourage the church to move beyond itself in the future. If we are to reenergize ourselves for the future, we must create a climate of holiness, an openness to God's Word and the anointive outpouring of the Holy Spirit, and a reemphasis on converting the church and its people by stressing saving souls, Bible literacy, and spiritual gifting.

Finally, we preachers need to recapture a sense of fun and adventure at work. These things help to energize us. Too many of us are uptight, unfriendly, and just downright unhappy. What happened to fun, adventure, and enjoyment in ministry? If we are miserable in our vocation, how are we to attract others? We must not take ourselves too seriously but relax and loosen up a bit. Is your church a place of fun, laughter, fellowship, and enjoyment for the people of God? Or are you staid, stiff, and stagnant, unable to free yourself into a spirit of joy and empowerment? When all spiritual gifts are allowed to flourish, there is a sense of fun, excitement, and adventure in ministry because of raised expectations about what God will do. When we try to control every outcome—create a climate where all gifts cannot flourish— we diminish divine expectations and sever our lifeline to God.

SUMMARY

Mainline Protestantism cannot afford to dismiss or negate the value of the more charismatic gifts of the Holy Spirit. If spiritual revitalization is to truly occur in the soul of the church, local churches must understand their role in creating and sustaining the spiritual milieu where all gifts are welcomed, nurtured, and sustained. By not recognizing the value of all spiritual gifts and by not incorporating those gifts into the life and ethos of the church, mainline churches undermine their capacity to grow and develop themselves in accordance with the will and trajectory of the Holy Spirit. Spiritual gifts precipitate the manifestation of spiritual fruit. Spiritual fruits are signs of God's continuing favor and power in the life of congregations.

5

RECLAIMING THE IMPORTANCE OF SPIRITUAL FORMATION

Most of our conflicts and difficulties come from trying to deal with the spiritual and practical aspects of our life separately instead of realizing them as parts of one whole.

—*Evelyn Underhill*

We must reclaim the importance of spiritual formation and the development of spiritual discipline as a basis for spiritual empowerment. Discipline influences discipleship. The Greek word for disciple is *mathetes,* which means "learner." A disciple is one who not only follows Christ, but is also one who is open to learning about Christ. As I mentioned previously, many of those in leadership positions in the church do not read their Bibles, have not established a consistent devotional life, and are not in spiritual formation. One of the great elements of the early Methodist movements was the emphasis on spiritual discipline through the development of a personal devotional life consisting of prayer and Bible study. This discipline was taught in classes where people met in the homes of various people for Bible study and prayer.

One of the great achievements of the early Christian movement was the emphasis on spiritual discipline as a foundation for spiritual empowerment and belief. The teaching of spiritual discipline constituted the backbone of the early ministries of Christian education. Early leaders taught people how to develop a devotional life, how to study the Bible, and how to pray. Every person in the church should be in spiritual formation or studying to show themselves approved in God's work. When we are not in spiritual formation and striving to learn and grow more in Christ, are we saying that we know all that we need to know for Christian service? If we are saying that we know all that we need to know for service, are we playing God? Every Christian should be diligently, actively, and meticulously seeking Christ by expanding his or her knowledge of God's word. This requires a spirit of confession, repentance, and humility. It means acknowledging that I don't know all I need to know to serve God effectively. It means shunning a spirit of arrogance that says I don't have to study, and instead learning and nurturing the Spirit to be a servant of Christ.

Christ was always teaching his disciples so that they were always in spiritual formation. They were always learning something new and applying themselves in different ways. A disciple is one who not only follows Christ, but is also one who is open to discovering more of Christ. Christ himself was always in spiritual formation by being open to new and fresh revelations from the Lord. How could he teach new and old truths without having read the Torah and without being open to learn new things that would positively affect his ministry for others?

Even after all of the formal education I have received and twenty years of ministry, I have discovered how much I don't know. Clergy, laity, and denominational prelates should all be actively seeking God's presence in spirit, love, and truth. We all should be open to learning more about Jesus and the workings of the Holy Spirit and be engaged in continual spiritual formation as an adventure. In order to learn more, we must believe the things we teach and preach. We must believe in the efficacy and transformative power of God's Word and the Holy Spirit.

It is an insult to believe that leaders who do not qualify themselves to lead spiritually in God's church can be optimally effective. In every other field of endeavor, the student must study and qualify himself or herself to lead or do work in a specific area or discipline. In the church we say, "whosoever will, let him come," and we do not challenge him or her to develop spiritual discipline and grow spiritually—and this is often our undoing. Leaders are often elected, but what in fact qualifies them to lead, other than their work experience in the secular world? Do they seek God's kingdom? Do they study God's Word? Are they in spiritual formation? Have they cultivated spiritual discipline? As outlined in *The Empowerment Church* (Nashville: Abingdon Press, 2001), every church should implement a Christian Training Academy that teaches the fundamentals of spiritual discipline, developing a devotional life, and understanding the power of prayer.

FORMING LEADERS

People who expect to lead in the church should have a humble spirit and a willingness to learn. Trumpeter Wynton Marsalis once remarked that his grandmother taught him, "There is a board for every behind." If you don't learn the easy way, you will learn the hard way. Arrogant people who don't humble themselves before God will often learn the hard way if they ever learn at all. "Pride goeth before the fall" and every leader should be seeking greater knowledge of himself, others, and Christ.

Every church leader and layperson should be actively and aggressively involved in spiritual formation by actively developing and strengthening their lives spiritually. The church is primarily a spiritual and faith community. Its leaders should know something about the Christian faith and model spirituality to the larger church and community. Spiritual formation will help leaders become spiritually centered and equip them with the knowledge and resources they need to empower others to develop a closer relationship with God. Spiritual formation means that leaders should not only attend leadership training sessions, but also diligently engage in Bible study, devotion, prayer, or other disciplines which will enhance and empower them spiritually.

One problem with leadership in some churches, as mentioned previously, is Bible illiteracy and the lack of spiritually informative programs designed to help leaders spiritually grow. Leaders should take seriously their leadership positions; a back to basics movement is necessary to rebuild the church into a viable community. How often do you pray? How often do you just have a little talk with Jesus? Is God a part of your daily conversation or just an afterthought or a 911 resource every time you get into trouble? How do you feel about people when the only time you hear from them is when they are in trouble or need something from you? I wonder how God feels about us when the only time we call is when we want something or are in need. If I am talking with God every day I don't need to call in special circumstances because spiritual formation tells me that God's already there!

Leaders who are called to lead should have a knowledge not only of church bylaws but also of the Bible. They should know how to conduct a meeting as well as how to pray to God. If the leaders in the spiritual community do not exemplify genuine spirituality, how is the church to move forward spiritually? Why do "Robert's or Mary's rules of order" take precedence over God's rules of order? For some people, all they know is Robert's or Mary's rules and not the golden rules for service in the church. Consider these questions:

- Do your leaders read the Bible? Do they attend worship service? Are they actively modeling spirituality in the larger congregation and community? Do they tithe? Do they attend meetings? Are they committed in their service to Christ and to the church?

- Do denominational officials stress the importance of spiritual formation? Do bishops, presiding elders, and others teach, preach, and reach spiritually? Do the daily rounds and demands of the institutional hierarchy create denominational leaders who appear to be more concerned with maintaining institutions than ostensibly modeling the way of Christian spirituality? Are denominational leaders cloyed and frustrated with church bureaucracy, to the point that they cannot lead as spiritually as they would like?

- If a primary frustration of pastors is the time consumed by administration, and not in doing things that are spiritually empowering to nurture the souls of their parishioners, do bishops and other leaders experience the same frustration in trying to spiritually lead their conferences and denominations?

Unfortunately, the absence of programs for spiritual formation of the church has done much to kill the church. All leaders should be required to engage in spiritual formation so they might be in the best mind for spiritual decision making as well as in support of the church and its ministries.

Together both pastors and laity should design programs of spiritual formation for leadership training and development. Establishing spiritual criteria for service in the church, such as attending Bible study, leadership training classes, or other

51

forms of spiritual discipline and devotion, will do much to empower the church's ministry.

STANDING ON THE PROMISES AND SITTING ON THE PREMISES

"Standing on the promises and sitting on the premises" suggests a kind of paradox. How can one sit and stand at the same time? We can stand in our thinking and sit in our action. We can stand in our beliefs and sit in our service. We can become the victims of a double indemnity; a spiritual ambiguity that leaves us more confused and tired than full of fire and energy that will propel us and others to Christian service. Spiritual formation for those serving in the church's institutional hierarchy is also important. How often do bishops and other denominational officials have an opportunity to replenish their souls or to lead retreats having to do with spiritual formation? Too often church officials are preoccupied with the business of running the conference or denomination and are themselves in desperate need of spiritual revitalization. How can denominational officials get the healing they need when they are immersed in and cloyed by the church's structures and machinery twenty-four hours a day, seven days a week? Papers, appointments, meetings that meet before other meetings are tired, boring, and rehash the same old stuff. Denominational officials find themselves caught in the spin cycle of denominational wheel work. T. S. Eliot said it best, "only a fool, fixed in his folly, may think he can turn the wheel on which he turns."

Church officials need to discard and delegate some of this stuff so they can do more teaching, preaching, and reaching for those souls inside and outside of the church. Bishops should be leading spiritual retreats, conducting altar calls and Bible studies at conferences, transversing their circuits to bring a good word from on high. Denominational leadership can be a kind of Babylonian captivity; exile to the paper land rather than a sojourn to the promised land. Pastors and laity look to their denominational leaders for spiritual leadership. Instead, they sometimes get overworked and underappreciated leaders who thankfully manage the chaos of the "memocracies" they lead, but have no time for spiritual revitalization themselves.

Denominational officials need a coming out of the bureaucratic morass so they can feel spiritually healthy and whole again. This means that the institutional wheelwork and machinery should be decentralized or turned over to independent, Christ-centered management companies who can manage the church day-to-day and denominational leaders can thus be freed up to do more in the area of spiritual revitalization within the places they have been called to serve. Spiritual formation should be the hallmark of every aspect of the ministry in mainline Protestant denominations. The following are ways to develop an environment of spiritual formation and discipline in the congregation:

1. Pray and ask God to renew and revitalize our fervor for service. Invoke the presence and power of the Holy Spirit in decision making for service.

2. Revitalize our daily walk with Christ by establishing a consistent devotional life. This devotional life should consist of prayer, praise, and celebration of the living and risen Christ. A strong and consistent devotional life leads to spiritual discipline and power. We develop our spiritual reflexes through the discipline of daily devotion.

3. Become open to the outpouring of God's renewing and refreshing spirit by inviting the Holy Ghost into church life.

4. Seek ways to be more creative and innovative in ministry. Try looking at a problem from a

different angle. Approach the problem with enthusiasm, humor, or some other positive quality. Take a more creative perspective and outlook on the methods by which the church ministers to others.

5. Surround yourself with people who have a joy and passion for service. Stop devoting time to the dead. As Jesus said, "Let the dead bury the dead." Associate with people who have fun, who like to laugh, who have a sense of humor, a sense of adventure, and a joy for service.

6. Take recreation time for your family, and for just yourself.

7. Keep hope, faith, and optimism alive in all things. Remember that whatever you are going through is not a permanent condition. Saint Sadie Mae said, "Scriptures say it came to pass which means it didn't come to stay."

8. Relinquish the details of denominational business to management services so officials can spend more time in spiritual formation by leading their people in spiritual nurturing and development.

SUMMARY

Reclaiming spiritual formation as a foundation for ministry suggests that we reclaim the fundamentals of disciplined devotion and study as spiritual practice. As seekers and builders of the kingdom of God, we must develop the spiritual discipline that leads to a consistent and regulated devotional life. A regulated devotional life provides believers with the knowledge and discipline that will empower their lives spiritually. Overcoming the obstacles and hardships that prevent our continual seeking and knowing God will have value in overcoming other impediments that keep us from growing in Christ through his church. By mastering the impediments that keep us from personal devotion, we master the larger obstacles that prevent our progress as a faith community.

We cannot become spiritually well and whole without taking seriously the imperatives of personal spiritual development. We must practice the faith and the discipline of spirituality that allows that faith to have practical meaning and value in today's world. Without spiritual formation, individual believers do not grow in their awareness of Christ and the church does not grow in its capacity to effect and sustain meaningful change in the lives of believers and the world. Mainline Protestantism must stress the importance of spiritual formation as a necessity for spiritual growth and effective leadership in the church of the future.

6
RECLAIMING OUR HISTORICAL LEGACY

In a dead religion there are no more heresies.

—Andre Suares

We must reclaim our denominational historical legacy. Now many people may take issue with this, but there is an identity crisis in mainline Protestantism. People simply do not know their history. Many of the answers to our present problems can be found in our past. Too many people lack knowledge of their history and thus feel they have to reinvent the wheel in order to make progress in the church.

Many mainline Protestant churches began as vital, spirit-filled movements, but as those denominations became more hierarchical and institutional, the organization priorities in maintaining and servicing vitality that originally spawned these movements dissipated. Many mainline churches want to become more spiritual, but how do they reconcile the spontaneity and power of the Holy Spirit with the need to maintain church structures and order? The overwhelming needs and presence of maintaining and sustaining a mammoth church bureaucracy can often eclipse the focus on spiritual vitality. By revisiting its historical legacy, the church can refresh and reinvigorate itself for service in the present context.

The problem is that many people run around setting the agenda for the local church, claiming to be experts on what is and what is not "denominationally correct" and "appropriate" and they are largely ignorant of church history. Oftentimes, they think that everything that is wooden and mechanical is denominational, while everything that teems with spiritual life and vitality is not. This belief runs counter to the revival spirit and evangelical impulse of the early denominational movements. However, this is a long-held misconception by many people. In actuality, many denominations began as a revival, Holy Ghost, spirit-filled, God-anointed movements where souls were set on fire for Christ, where the preacher preached and the teachers taught, and the leaders reached out into the community to bring lost and forlorn souls the good news of the risen Christ.

For many years, I have had an ongoing concern about the decline and closure of black churches in particular and mainline Protestant churches in general. It is amazing that a church can decline, disintegrate, and go out of business when there are still so many yet unsaved. One writer stated that if we were to line up all the unchurched people in the world into a single file, that line would extend around the world at least seven times.

Further perplexing is how many churches have descended into a kind of spiritual malaise and atrophy where the Body of Christ appears to be strangely afflicted, wasting away, or dying of a deadly cancer that is eating away at its core, thus bringing suffering, and sudden, certain death. Much of this decline can be ascribed to the development of habits, beliefs, and practices that have precipitated the spiritual decline of those churches. Much of this decline can also be ascribed to aging churches who have lost energy and zeal with the aging process, coupled with a refusal to change and do something new. As Daniel Buttry reminds us in *Bringing Your Church Back to Life: Beyond Survival Mentality*, their preoccupation is with survival and keeping the doors open and what holds them together is the memory of the good old days rather than the prospect of a realizable future.

No one wants to be a part of an organization, church, or group that is thanatoid, necrophilic, or downright dead. Many people have been tricked into believing that the quieter the worship the more true to the denomination. There is nothing wrong with quiet, contemplative worship, but do I have to be quiet all the time? Can't I shout or openly express praise and joy for what Christ has done in my life some of the time?

This problem is particularly acute in some churches where the "Denominationally Correct Police" show up flashing their official badges warning others to be quiet when they want to praise and celebrate the risen Lord! Their interest is more in maintaining order and control in the name of the denominational correctness than in allowing the Holy Spirit to come into service and have its way. Moreover, these so-called officials are not even historically correct, because if they knew their history, they would understand that shouting in worship or openly expressing oneself in praise and celebration was a hallmark of many denominations' beginnings. That's why we need to reclaim our historical legacy in order to claim a viable future.

Reclaiming our historical legacy does not mean that we have to do everything today exactly as it was done yesterday. It means reclaiming those vital traditions of yesterday to help revitalize the church today.

The irony is that many mainline churches began as evangelical, Holy Ghost–filled movements that won souls to Christ and which gave denominations a fervor and fire unrivaled by any Christian group. In looking at many of these churches now, they are listless and lifeless, mausoleums for the spiritually dead rather than coliseums of praise and celebration for a living and risen Christ. Rather than possessing true spiritual vitality which was once the proud hallmark of these churches, we now have deadpan churches with deadpan services.

These various evangelical movements which were once spiritually robust and vital have aspects that now have devolved into spiritually anemic institutions that have lost their power of discipleship and witness, are not open to the teaching and guidance of the Holy Ghost, and are devoid of spiritual gifts and graces. Many of these churches have developed cultures and traditions that are contrary to the original vision of their founders and thus we now have churches that have become so steeped in their own individual traditions, modes of governance, and cultures that they have lost sight of their larger spiritual reason for being, which is saving souls, transforming lives and communities, and calling the people back to God.

For instance, John Wesley would turn over in his grave if he knew how Methodist churches and other Protestant churches have forsaken the spiritual rudiments of the Christian faith and have lost their evangelical fire and fervor. These early movements did not begin as the highly institutionalized, bureaucratic organizations they have come to be, but as living organisms, life transforming, grassroots movements begun by reformers and revolutionaries of the faith who used their minds and spirits to glorify God.

The Wesleyan movement, in particular, was a Holy Ghost movement that the Pentecostal Church, Church of God, and other charismatic and evangelical movements claim as part of their parental heritage.

One problem with the American evangelical movement as Richard Hoftstader and Mark Noll, in separate works, have observed is that many of the movements lost their evangelical emphasis because of the anti-intellectualism of the American evangelical movement. In an effort to divorce or separate themselves from the anti-intellectualism of the

American evangelical movement, many of these denominations lost the spiritual zeal that won them early success on the American frontier. The problem is fundamentalism's literal interpretation of the Bible and a perceived narrowing of consciousness. The image of fundamentalism in the American evangelical movement has turned off many progressive students of enlightenment thinking. Rather than a new fundamentalism, we need a new foundationalism that values and practices those basic principles of the faith that create spiritually healthy churches. Foundationalism understands the necessities of living and trafficking in secular society, appropriates some aspects of secular society, but is not spiritually or theologically compromised, or overwhelmed by secular society.

The architects of these early movements, such as Martin Luther, John Wesley, and Jonathan Edwards, were not only great minds who resolved some of the most perplexing doctrinal problems of their time and thus used their minds to glorify God, but also they were not apologetic about spirituality. They believed in the fundamentals and foundational principles of the Christian faith. They were not ashamed of the power and working of the Holy Ghost in their lives. They brought together the best of both worlds: intellect and spirit. They stressed the importance of being born again, having a conversion experience, and claimed the Bible as the quintessential authority of the Christian faith.

The other problem is that secular humanism and modern paganism have unduly influenced the church's selling out to and accommodation of popular culture and secular society. As clergy and laity in mainline Protestant churches became more middle class, educated, and economically well-off, they renounced the inherent anti-intellectualism of the American evangelical movement, and by so doing, dissociated themselves from some of the more vital tenets of faith.

Perhaps it was for this reason, when The Methodist Church united with The Evangelical United Brethren Church in 1968, the church took the new name "The United Methodist Church" instead of "The Methodist Evangelical Church." Did the church want to avoid the anti-intellectual, "primitive," and "fundamental" associations that the word, "Evangelical," suggests? However, it is precisely this name—barring the more dubious association created by the word "evangelical"—that would have given The United Methodist Church more appeal in the modern charismatic age. The point here is that many mainline denominations have shunned their evangelical heritage which was once an integral part of church life and tradition and helped them build strong churches in the past. Evangelical is something we aren't anymore. All these outward, expressive, celebrative models of ecclesiastical conduct are archaic, obsolete, out-of-date, and beneath the sophistication and dignity we are called to maintain. For some, getting too evangelical is becoming too narrow-minded and getting "ugly" for Jesus; losing control of oneself under the unction and anointing of the Holy Spirit is unquestionably primitive! The task then is to shun, avoid, and discard the label of being too evangelical because being too evangelical means being too uncritical, too unthoughtful, too unsophisticated, too primitive, too literal, and too fundamental for our enlightened sensibilities. However, being evangelical is a positive expression of faith and spirituality and we should not be ashamed to claim it as part of our heritage.

The same is true of the Baptists, Anabaptists, Lutherans, and other denominational movements. The difference is that Baptists have retained more of their evangelical identity personified by a general openness to the movement and power of the Holy Ghost, celebrative worship experiences, church polity, and general styles of governance that are more conducive to leaders and followers in the charismatic and evangelical traditions. It is also true that Baptists have appealed more to the spiritual and evangelical sensibilities of black Americans because their styles of worship, leadership culture, and basic doctrines are more evangelical.

SUMMARY

Regrettably, many churches have lost a broader spiritual appeal to the black and white masses because they have failed to evaluate and examine their current relevancy and have failed to develop new styles and modalities of worship, church culture, and governance that speak to modern generations. This truth can be applied to all mainline Protestant denominations including the Baptist, Presbyterian, Lutheran, Episcopalian, United Churches of Christ, and Methodist traditions. However, if these denominations would make a more concerted effort to know, reclaim, and celebrate their histories, they would reacquire some of the spiritual vitality they are lacking today. By reclaiming the vital parts of their historical legacies, they would avoid delegitimation by those forces and powers who want to label their expressive evangelical styles as not authentic and true to their denominational legacies. In the case of traditions of those mainline denominations who do not have a more evangelical or charismatic heritage, it may be wise for them to appropriate some aspects of it for the new age as they reconfigure themselves and fashion a new, more appealing identity to the masses. If spiritual revitalization in mainline churches is to occur, they should take seriously the evangelical legacies of their past. Those evangelism paradigms that worked in the past can have meaning and value for present and future generations.

7

RECLAIMING A PASSION FOR PREACHING

He that has but one Word of God before him, and out of that Word cannot make a sermon, can never be a preacher.
—*Martin Luther*

Gardner Taylor once remarked that if we were to discover the reasons for the death of the Christian church we would discover that the sermon had killed it. Many mainline churches have lost spiritual vitality because the preaching is, quite frankly, listless and dead. The messenger is tired and the message is more tired. One criticism I received in seminary was that my sermons were not conversational in tone. There is nothing wrong with conversation from the pulpit, but that talk should not be without passion and energy.

One minister's wife complained that her husband's sermons were so boring that they put his parishioners to sleep, "All right," he said, "I'll tape myself and play it back after today's sermon." Five minutes into the sermon the wife found her

65

husband fast asleep in his study. So boring was he that he put himself to sleep. It is one thing for the preacher to talk in his or her own sleep, but God help the preacher who talks in the sleep of his parishioners during Sunday service.

For some churches, the "great awakening" is when the minister finishes his sermon in Sunday worship. Small wonder that many mainline churches have lost spiritual vitality. Even more problematic is that many students go through divinity school and seminary having never taken one course on homiletics. Moreover, numerous homiletics professors do not hone their craft each Sunday.

Boredom and tired preaching are the bane of some ministries today. "How shall they hear without a preacher?" How shall they be comforted, convicted, and converted without one who preaches with passion, fire, or enthusiasm? Many of the great preachers of old were in the mainline church. Phillips Brooks, Harry Emerson Fosdick, and Gerald Kennedy were ministers in mainline denominations and today, Gardner Taylor, Frederick Sampson, James Earl Massey and others are ministers in mainline denominations. What happened to the passion for preaching and sermon preparation?

True, the nature of preaching has changed over the years but nothing can substitute for good, solid, passionate biblical preaching. Unfortunately, too many churches have gone wanting in this area. How shall we convict through God's Word if we ourselves have not been convicted? How shall we energetically and joyfully preach salvation if we have not been saved? When John Wesley asked Peter Böhler what should he do if he preached without faith, Böhler's reply was, "Preach faith until you have it."

People today often use the expression, "I can feel you." In other words, I can sense what you are feeling inside of me. "I feel your pain" and "I feel your joy" are expressions that are rooted in our capacity to sense life on a deeper visceral level with others. Similarly, the audience should feel what the preacher is feeling; passion is vital in the communication of ideas. People should not only experience the preached Word cerebrally (with the head), but also viscerally (with the heart and soul).

Soul force is essential in passionate preaching—the capacity for the soul to express itself honestly and openly in the preaching venue. The preacher should feel what he or she is preaching. The audience should connect emotionally and psychologically with both message and messenger.

To preach in a detached, dispassionate manner is often to invite disbelief. The listener asks, does the preacher really believe what he or she is preaching? Is she or he convinced of the efficacy of the gospel message? Is his or her belief communicated in the passion and confidence of what he or she says as well as how he or she says it? Does the preacher manifest this passionate belief in his or her walk and talk? Does he or she evidence the passion of belief in relation to others?

All good preaching expresses belief on a level that resonates with listeners. Feeling what you believe and expressing it openly and honesty will do much to convince people to Christ. Boring, ill-prepared, matter-of-fact, "ain't got nothing and don't want nothing" preaching is an anathema to the church. People can stay home and be bored. They can hear conversation while doing other things. They can derive more excitement from being in the world at a stadium or concert hall than in having their time wasted listening to insipid, meaningless preaching. People have better things to do with their time than be bored by preachers who themselves would find more enjoyment doing other things.

True, as servants of God we all periodically exemplify a tiredness that comes from being stretched too thin, for having too little time in the study, or in doing the things we enjoy most. Ministry places enormous demands on us that zap our energy and quench our fires for service. This we understand.

What I am referring to is a general tiredness and lethargy that is normative, that is part of the "business as usual," hohum, rhythm and cycle of church ministry. In this situation, everything we do for Christ is tired. Our liturgies are tired. Our praying is tired. We are ensconced in a culture of blessed tiredness. So we go about our little tired rituals in the same old monolithic, monotone ways; we speak dispassionately and we wonder why people stay away from the church. They would much rather be around rowdy friends who are whooping it up and having a good time than tired church folk and tired preachers. "Blessed are the tired for we shall not convince them to Christ," should be a sign on the study doors of some preachers.

I don't mean to be cynical here but maybe that's why Martin Luther once said, "I have been around these good Christians so long that I long for the company of honest-to-God sinners." Sinners are never boring. They have fun, life, and enthusiasm. There is never a dull moment in their company. But these tired Christians with their tired songs and ways kill any vestige of enthusiasm for Christ. We need to learn how to jazz things up, get pep in our step, glide in our stride. Some white people should study aspects of some black culture and learn how to get some feeling and passion for what they do for God. Some black people should study aspects of their own culture and learn how to get some fire in their bones for preaching. Blacks and whites who are boring in their sermon preparation and delivery should study the dynamic aspects of black culture and black spirituality, and white Southern culture and spirituality.

Tired preaching and tired preachers have helped to kill mainline Protestantism. **We must claim and reclaim a passion for preaching.** We should preach in a way that people can feel us, feel Jesus, and feel the blessed, transformative power of the Holy Spirit. You don't have to swing from the lights or do acrobats in the pulpit to passionately convey the gospel message. It may mean something as simple as changing the tone of one's voice, of feeling the words or ideas spoken rather than uttering them in a wooden, half-hearted manner. That passion can be expressed in a reverberant shout or in a still, small whisper. The point is to have some feeling when we are preaching. We don't have to become so emotional that we completely lose control or so cerebral that we impede the passionate flow of ideas. Somewhere in the middle is a happy medium where we can genuinely express ourselves in ways that garner people's attention and interest and motivate them to Christ.

Whatever it takes to reclaim that passion, we must do it. This passion is not endemic to young versus old or black versus white. It's about what we feel as citizens of the world and laborers for the kingdom of God. It's really about what Christ means to you, how you feel about Christ, and how you want to share him with others. For example, my preaching witnesses to my genuine, dialogical relationship with Christ—a relationship filled with pain and suffering, joy and sweet relief. I want to tell others of his goodness and mercy, his resurrection power and amazing grace, and this requires a certain amount of passion in my preaching. Passion often comes through suffering. We must study the larger culture to learn how to effectively communicate ideas. Drama, gestures, and various pitches invigorate preaching. Whatever you do, don't be tired, dull, and lifeless in your preaching context and delivery.

SUMMARY

Until mainline Protestantism can shun the label of being tired and boring, and until preachers can gain more passion in their preaching, mainline churches will continue their slow, steady, lethargic decline into the abyss of no return. If we are going to revive mainline Protestantism, we must reemphasize the importance of passionately conveying the kerygma. Nothing will substitute for good, sound, passionate biblical preaching for lost souls in a dying world!

If we are to proclaim the gospel to a dying world and convince people to Christ within that world, we must preach with fervor, feeling, and fire. We must exhort the word of

God with passion, privilege, and power. The recovery of passionate preaching can mean the recovery of the soul of the preacher as well as those lost souls in the world. Passion for preaching is a positive step in revitalizing the messenger as well as the message in a generation that has heard it all before. Boring preaching kills enthusiasm. Passionate preaching incites life, vitality, and enthusiasm for Christ, his church, and the ministry. How shall they believe if the messenger does not exemplify the passion of belief in the message?

8

RECLAIMING THE PURPOSE OF THE CHURCH

The church is not a gallery for the exhibition of eminent Christians, but a school for the education of imperfect ones.

—*Henry Ward Beecher*

The church's purpose is connected to the church's image. What is the image of your church among parishioners and the larger, immediate community? Is your church a museum where nothing is preserved but memories of the past and thus you are living solely in that past? Is your church a country club only for the elite and others who think like you and look like you? Is your church a massage parlor where the whole purpose is to comfort, massage, and make people feel good? Is it a nursing home for the elderly, or a place where the young in heart and spirit are not welcomed or invited? What is the image of your church? Hospital for the sick and afflicted? Recreational center for the lost and lonely? Image is strongly related to purpose. How I imagine my church will largely shape my understanding of the church's purpose and the church's purpose will help shape its image. What is the church's fundamental purpose? What is the purpose of your church in your local context? How is this purpose being conveyed, taught, and disseminated? What is your church's profile in the community? Cold, friendly, accessible, aloof? Do you concur with Robert Frost's statement that good fences make good neighbors and that's why there is a fence or wall around your church to keep parishioners in and the community out? **Every church must reclaim both a program of spiritual uplifting and empowerment for the people of God, and a program of communal uplifting and empowerment for the people who live in its community.**

Has a culture of narcissism prevailed in the church, where the church seems more concerned with looking inward and tending to denominational structures than with looking outward and developing community-based programs for empowerment and service? Many churches have lost their umbilical ties to the communities in which they are located and rely upon the denomination to carry out their mission needs in the global community. In other words, many churches have lost their sense of presence and participation in the life of communities and do not address the ultimate concerns of those communities. Thus churches have no ministries that speak to real relationships with the community they are called to serve. Just being physically there is not enough. The church must make its presence known and felt in the community in which it is called to witness.

INVESTMENT OF SELF

One basic presupposition for ministry is the willingness to commit oneself to faithful service to Christ. The investment of self requires submission to God and the surrender of self to be used by the Holy Spirit for service to the community. *Kenosis* connotes the total outpouring or release of the self into something higher and vital. Christ poured out himself for us that we might have a more abundant life. God continually pours out the Holy Spirit for us as we seek to serve his people in ministry. This *kenosis,* or outpouring, is a source of our strength.

Investment also suggests a willingness to be used by the Holy Spirit to make the church better than we found it by improving its quality of life. Too often, we simply find ourselves maintaining the status quo. While maintaining a church is better than making it worse, a more beneficial approach would be to transform the church through a personal investment of time, intellect, talent, and resources. Reclaiming the purpose of the church means clarifying our role and responsibility in its mission and ministry. Ask yourself:

- Are you giving yourself completely to God to be used as God wills?

- How invested are you in serving?

- Are your body, mind, soul, and spirit present with you in your service to the church?

- How invested are you in the community and culture of the people where your congregation is located?

- What plans do you have for a long-term investment in building your church's ministry?

- Are there concerns, issues, or problems that might preclude your full investment in ministry? If so, identify these issues and discuss them with other leaders.

- What can you do to move from divestment to investment?

VISION

Do you know who your church is and where it is going? Does your church have a vision which is not only consistent with the larger denomination but with the people and community it serves? Has your church written a three- to five-year pastor's, lay, or strategic vision plan for your congregation? Where does your church hope to be in two, three, or five years? What resources will you mobilize and what is your action plan for getting there?

One central problem with clergy and churches in denominational systems is the manner in which the larger church's vision overshadows or obviates the local church's vision of who it is and where it should go. Each congregation should have both a vision of the larger church's expectation for itself, and a vision of its own expectation of how it will carry out both the denominational and local mission. The larger denomination and local church's vision should have common elements, but the local church should also have some understanding of how it will minister to local communities.

Each congregation should have a vision statement which is based on the real needs of the people in the church and larger community. How can pastors and others viably lead when they haven't the faintest clue of where they are going? What is your vision? *Why* is it your vision? When is your vision to occur? Where is your vision taking place? How is your vision working? What are the time lines and processes you will employ to bring your vision to fruition?

As a Boy Scout, I once experienced being led by someone who didn't know where he was going. A fellow Scout and close friend decided to lead us on a midnight expedition looking for the infamous bloody bones. We proceeded to sneak out precisely at midnight, being led by our fearless leader who "knew" where he was going. Some other troopers knew the route we would be taking at midnight and had removed the outhouse from its hole earlier that evening.

Need I say where we ended up? He may have known where he was going but he had no vision of where we would end up. Our falling in the latrine became legendary among Michigan state Boy Scout troops and gave us all a lesson in leadership we never forgot: Always have a vision of not only your destination, but also the means and paths to getting there.

Vision requires *imagination*. Churches need imaginative leaders and ministries that dare to think and do as never before. Leaders who lack vision and imagination are like planes without wings and cars without wheels. Visions are dynamic. They help to move things to their appointed and anointed place. They inspire people to move beyond their own barriers and constraints to embrace a reality that is much larger and greater than themselves. Visions inspire community building and fellowship, which are two essential ingredients to successful congregations.

Leaders should have a vision of where the congregation is going. Nehemiah had a vision of rebuilding the wall of Jerusalem. He imagined how the previous wall looked, but he embellished the new wall with visions of his own that made it even greater than the previous wall.

One thing that demobilizes congregations and ministries is a lack of vision and purpose. All churches should be engaged in some building or rebuilding activity. There's too much work for churches to be idle. A vision provides a blueprint for the future. If you fail to plan, you plan to fail. In order to create a vision you must:

1. Convene a group of laity to formulate a vision or strategic plan. Spend months establishing and clarifying that vision. Make plans to develop a written vision statement. (It is important to not only have traditionalists but also visionary and creative people on this committee. The direction you will be going will not only embrace the past but also

anticipate the future. You want people who have a feel for tradition, but also people who can envision the church and ministry creatively.)

2. Develop time lines and frameworks for the vision to be established and implemented and plan to present it to the larger church for endorsement.

3. Make sure your vision is not something that simply grows out of your own head. Sit where the people sit and develop a vision that represents God's vision, yours views, and their views. Too often leaders develop their visions in a vacuum. It must be based on the real or perceived needs of the people, culture, and community of the church and something that people can readily buy, own, and embrace.

SAVING SOULS AND EMPOWERING LIVES

Every denomination has theological foundations that inform its basic systems of belief. Theology will often influence the nature and trajectory of ministries within those denominations. Notwithstanding variations in theology, each church or denomination should organize itself around the basic idea of saving souls and empowering lives. The church is in God's business of helping people live more wholesome and spirit-filled lives, to nurture and develop their spirituality so they might attain wholeness, vitality, and wellness, and to translate that spirit of awareness into meaningful acts of grace and empowerment in society. The church's purpose is to call the people back to God; to point them to God's continuing revelation and presence in our times, and to give continuing witness to the Lordship of Jesus Christ.

Many churches have lost the idea of saving souls as their fundamental purpose. In the early days of many mainline denominations, soul saving was understood to be a fundamental purpose of the church's mission and ministry and was one reason why many of those churches experienced such phenomenal growth. The church preached, taught, and modeled what it meant to be saved, but unfortunately, the reality of being saved seems not so popular anymore.

Have mainline churches lost a basic understanding of their fundamental purpose which is to make disciples of all nations and to share the power of the risen Christ with a dying world? Have the constraints of the modern, institutional, bureaucratic church eclipsed or distracted the local churches from saving souls?

From an institutional standpoint, the purpose of the church denomination may be to perpetuate existing structures in order to facilitate the ministries of local churches. We need institutions, but without soul saving in the local church which ultimately increases membership in local congregations, the larger church would cease to exist. The institutional apparatus of the larger denomination should facilitate ministry in local churches; many mainline denominations have done this quite well over the years. The question now is if souls are not being saved in local churches as they previously were during the more robust growth periods of denominational and membership growth, what will the future hold for those denominational structures? If souls are not being saved and lives are not being changed, could those structures one day become extinct? Has the tendency of denominational institutions to preoccupy themselves with bureaucratic maintenance, some of which is necessary and some of which isn't, caused local churches to become more focused on meeting the needs of the denominations than on saving souls in the communities they serve?

In United Methodism, we often talk of connectionalism; being linked to other churches and being umbilically tied to the parent organization of the church. This is a wonderful concept. The problem is that in our desire to be connected to each other within the church, we sometimes disconnect from the people and communities we are called to serve outside of the church. Once we disconnect from the people and communities we are called to serve it is difficult to develop the energy and establish those vital ties that will convince them for Christ. To be organically and spiritually connected both denominationally and communally is the best possible scenario. We can serve the denomination but not eliminate the need to serve the people of God through the local church. The truth is it is difficult to do both and often clergy find themselves torn between serving denominational structures and ministering in a local context. Because the demands of ministry are so enormous, and pastors often find themselves torn in so many impossible directions, denominational service can bring either relief or additional burdens. Notwithstanding these concerns, the basic purpose of the church is to save souls and transform lives for the glory of God. The more the church is able to get back to this fundamental purpose, the more it can be revitalized with new blood and a fresh anointing of the Holy Spirit.

As mainline denominations evaluate themselves and ask the tough questions, their purpose would be greater served if they could begin assessing the basic assumptions they have concerning their purpose and service. What is the primary purpose of denominational institutions? How might that purpose be clarified, revised, or changed entirely? Is the purpose of denominational structures to maintain themselves, to provide bureaucratic oversight to local churches and other denominational structures? To what extent does the denomination's current system hinder or enhance the ability of local churches to save souls and transform lives for Christ? Rather than preoccupy themselves with maintaining the church's status quo organizationally and bureaucratically, could those institutions and their personnel engage in soul saving on a larger institutional level which could empower churches to become more engaged in soul winning for Christ locally? Should all denominational officials and workers be trained in the principles of evangelism and witness, so that denominational structures may also engage in soul winning for Christ, rather than spending so much time tending to the organizational structures of the denomination?

The purpose of the church is to maintain and vouchsafe tradition but also to transform and be transformed for God's glory. To what degree do denominational structures model or impair this transformative process? Are institutions capable of transforming themselves, reinventing themselves, or reconfiguring themselves for a new day?

The church on all levels must have the courage to change and to be changed. It must go back to the fundamental purpose of its reason for being. Without new souls being saved, who will make up the new church? Where will the church be in the next twenty, thirty, or forty years? Saving souls and empowering lives is the fundamental purpose of the church on both the denominational and local church levels.

TRANSFORMING SELF, CHURCH, COMMUNITY, AND SOCIETY

The church is not only called to save souls through evangelizing and discipleship, those souls who are saved are called to give continuing witness to the saving and transforming power of Christ in the world. It is not enough for believers to be saved individually for themselves. It is not enough to have church, to get happy and get full of the Holy Ghost on Sundays and then not translate that awareness into creative energies that will positively transform the self, church, community, and the world. Through conversion, those who are saved develop a radical awareness of self, community, and society. This awareness is undergirded by the transforming grace of Christ himself and the power of the Holy Spirit. The church then should serve as a catalyst for the creative and positive transformation of those existing structures within the self, the church, community, society, and world that thwart person's capacities to actualize their potential and to experience wholeness, peace, and vitality. The church's purpose must also include bringing truth to power, and challenging systems of oppression and injustice that destroy lives. The church should be an agent for the positive and holistic transformation of self and society.

This transformation can be encouraged by the church's willingness to evaluate and transform itself and by modeling that change in ways that give hope to its members and to the larger community. Savings souls and enabling those souls to witness to, participate in, and ultimately transform the existing order for the good of all is an important purpose of the church and is one of the hallmarks of the ministry of Jesus Christ.

SUMMARY

The church's purpose is to share Christ in a way that will facilitate internal spiritual and external social transformation in a way that will give each person a sense of wholeness, vitality, justice, and peace. Transformation through Christ should be the primary purpose of the church. In order to transform, the church must be freed and transformed for this purpose.

By experiencing a deeper internal transformation by the Holy Spirit, mainline churches can externalize the power of that change into the positive transformation of the community and world. By being open to the leadership and guidance of the Holy Spirit, the church can always be in touch with its fundamental purpose which is saving souls and positively changing the world. The purpose of the church should be in sync with the purpose of the Father, Son, and Holy Ghost.

9

RECLAIMING THE MISSION OF THE CHURCH

The church which is not a missionary church will be a missing church when Jesus comes.

—F. B. Meyer

We must reclaim the mission of the church. We should ask ourselves: What is our fundamental mission? Who are we? Why are we? Where are we? How will we carry out the mission to the community and the larger world? We talk about getting horizontally connected as a denomination, but a larger question is: Are we vertically connected to the Lord in our mission and work? Is the church carrying out its mission? If not, why? Does the church need to corporately repent of its sins, shed excess baggage, and experience conversion so it can be freed to do ministry in the present age? Have leaders reclaimed their mission in ministry? Have they been converted to Christ? Are they following, leading, and staying out of God's way?

The church has many gifts and graces, but if congregations

and the larger church are to grow, revitalize, and renew themselves we must take the steps necessary to reclaim the mission of the church.

BACK TO THE FUTURE

By "back to the future" I mean retrieving those denominational mission elements of the past that make strong and viable churches in the future. For example, John Wesley issued the following warning in 1786: "I am not afraid that the people called Methodists should ever cease either in Europe or America. But I am afraid lest they should exist only as a dead sect, having the form of religion without the power."

When we speak of going back to the future we mean that we do not have to reinvent the wheel. We must learn something about that tradition and appropriate that tradition for church growth and renewal. We can learn much from Wesley and the early Methodists. We know that they went beyond the four walls of containment to evangelize persons to Christ. We know that they were on fire for Christ, that they preached the word with passion and zeal and braved many dangers on the American frontier during the Great Awakening. We know that their worship services were celebrative and anointed with the presence and power of the Holy Spirit.

Going back to the future means we appropriate the early emphasis on cultivating spiritual gifts for service—all gifts, that we stress the meaning of word centeredness and Bible literacy in our churches, that we demonstrate our faith in witness to the larger community, that we manifest a passion for Christ that translates into a passion for service to God's people. We know that Wesley traveled thousands of miles by horseback to reach souls for Christ, that he set up medical clinics that dispensed medicine to the poor and offered loans to the indigent. He did not have a wait-and-see attitude toward the gospel. Just as Jesus went out with a witness to the Word, so did Wesley, and so should we if we expect to grow.

When we have worship services that are celebrative and Holy Ghost–filled, and the anointing power of the spirit is present, we reclaim our mission by revisiting our denominational roots, where they preached, sang, shouted, prayed, and celebrated their lives in Christ with joy and power. We need to retrieve some of the early Wesleyan revival spirit as a means of planting seeds, nurturing the soil, and bringing forth fruit in our ministries and revitalizing dead churches.

The early church movements were not dead movements, and we too should be alive in Christ. The success of the early churches that emerged from the American evangelical movement was due in part to their joy for service. No one wants to be a part of a dead church, with dead worship services, dead preaching, dead singing, dead meetings, dead fellowship, dead Bible study, dead evangelism, cooking that's dead, and everything else dead. How can preachers ignite a fire on Sunday when they themselves have not been convinced to Christ, when the laity are not convinced, and have not had a saving, liberating, motivating relationship with Christ? Christ arose so that we as the church and people of God could rise from our graves of complacency, listlessness, and dispassion. He didn't stay in the grave. He got up from the grave and that's what mainline churches need to do as well.

Moreover, we need to bear fruit in our ministries. If we are sharing and bearing our gifts for Christ in ministry we should manifest fruit in ministry. We can reclaim our mission by emphasizing cultural fluency, word centeredness, prophetic consciousness, spiritual discipline, and evangelical outreach. There are approximately 262 million people in the United States and 187 million have yet to accept Jesus Christ. We still have much work ahead of us.

Biblically Based Mission

The mission of the church should coincide with the gospel. All missions should be biblically based. The church's mission is not only to preach and teach the gospel in a dying world but feed the hungry, clothe the naked, help heal the sick, visit the prisoners, and empower people in Christ. Jesus' mission to the poor, sick, afflicted, hungry, and oppressed is a missional model worthy of emulation.

Each congregation must have sense of its biblical mandates for mission in the world. Each denomination should have an understanding of its calling and mission to the local church as well as to the larger society. Mission that is biblically based takes seriously the mandate of the gospel to reach out and help those in need. This means helping people not only within the four walls of the church, but also ministering to people outside those walls. With whom do we share the mission? To whom do we direct the mission?

The Bible helps us to understand the mandates, importance, and purpose of our mission to the people of the world. Since the Bible is a primary authority and resource in our various traditions, it can help clarify our missional objectives as a faith community.

The Church in Mission to Itself

Should the church be in mission to itself? Given the current state of decline and challenge within mainline denominations, should those churches develop a mission that will enable them to overcome their present afflictions and problems? We seldom think of a church in mission to itself. We believe that a church in mission to itself is a selfish, myopic church. But why shouldn't a church be in mission to itself if it needs revitalization and overhauling? Shouldn't a portion of denominational resources be directed to a mission that will help the church to become healthy and well again? If the church itself is sick and in need of healing and wholeness, why wouldn't the healthier aspects of the church reach out to comfort and heal its sicker aspects?

Mission is not only to a world in need of the gospel of hope and love, but is also to the church itself. We think of mission as means of eradicating the world of poverty, hopelessness, and disease. But what about being in mission to eradicate spiritual poverty—poverty of the mind and soul that exists within the church?

In order to be revitalized, the church must be in mission to itself so that it can become well enough to minister to the world for Christ. The church itself must redefine the meaning of mission. There are parts of the church that need healing, wholeness, wellness, and a helping hand as much as the world needs these things. The church should not be afraid to confess its need to be in mission to itself so that it can become healthy and well enough to minister to the world.

THE CHURCH IN MISSION TO THE WORLD

Going beyond the four walls of the church is extremely important in helping others in need. John Wesley said it best when he exclaimed, "The world is my parish." The church must develop holy boldness to travel to every part of the world to witness for Christ and to help others in need. This means the global communities as well as local communities. It is highly paradoxical that the church should be in mission to the world—that it should brave dangers and hardships, and toil in the world community, but not be in mission to local communities. Where did we get the idea that we can be in mission to the global community but neglect our own communities that are often just as impoverished and underdeveloped as some Third World countries?

Mission work is laborious and rewarding work. The labors of missionaries are legendary in the annals of

Christendom. But shouldn't denominations also be in mission to local communities, communities that have been devastated by poverty, disease, and environmental concerns?

To be in mission to people in places like Africa and Bangladesh is very important. To be in mission to gang-infested, crime-ridden communities in Chicago and Detroit is equally important. The missional outreach to local communities can have denominational presence. Each denomination can have missional priorities in relation to the central cities or urban areas and the villages and towns of rural areas. Why couldn't there be a United Methodist, Episcopalian, Lutheran, or Presbyterian agency of relief in local communities? Undoubtedly each of these denominations has missions and helps people in need in those communities.

In what ways can denominations and churches partner cross-denominationally to share in mission outreach to certain local communities? In defining our mission to the world, we must include the local as well as global communities. The church must not only reach out to the world but also to those communities and societies in our own backyard who need help, hope, and wholeness. Why expend all of our resources abroad? Shouldn't charity also begin at home?

The point here is that the mission objectives of denominations seeking to revitalize themselves must also include local communities, and just as resources are harnessed and deployed in the development of Third World countries to help them come to Christ, our local mission must not only include feeding and housing and clothing persons, but also cultivating models of enterprise and redevelopment that will create new communities of hope in blighted and impoverished areas of this land.

A train ride to Dallas, Texas in October of 2001 opened my eyes to the devastating poverty in our nation. Because the rail system is shared by many other railway enterprises, a train can often stop in the middle of nowhere in order to give the right of way to other trains carrying passengers and freight. We had stopped for a half hour in a place in

Arkansas, and what I saw brought tears to my eyes. The poverty was so glaring it would make the projects in Chicago look like Beverly Hills. There was no electricity. Trailer homes had holes in their roofs. Those roofs were covered by pieces of plastic to shelter inhabitants from pouring rains. Acres of firewood sprawled everywhere. Children ran scantily clad amid rubble and debris, much of which were rusted out cars and other poisonous matter. In this one area was a pond that was certainly filled with fecal and other deadly matter. A child was flapping her small hand in the water. The smell was so malodorous that it penetrated the sealed windows of the train cars. This is America!

This place was worse than any foreign place I have ever visited. It seems that we must redefine the meaning of our mission to the world. This world beside the train tracks must also include our world—the world of not only urban America, but also rural America—the world of not only black people but white people and any other people whose life is steeped in the quagmires of poverty, desolation, and despair. It is almost criminal that the government should spend billions on weapons, corporate bailouts, and warfare while its own citizens die of malnutrition and disease at epidemic proportions. What is the church doing about this? Why should we be in mission abroad when our own country is going to hell?

Mainline denominations may have to redefine the meaning of mission by not only reaching out to those in need globally but also locally. The responsibilities for this outreach must rest on more than the local church. Resources must be cultivated to eradicate poverty, disease, hopelessness, and despair on all levels of our society and world. To preach and teach Christ globally means also to share that good news locally. It also means engaging in missional projects that will eliminate all forms of hopelessness and hunger in our world. The church must speak to these concerns. Poverty and hunger still rage in America. While large corporations consolidate and expand their profits in global markets, people die of hunger and disease right here in America.

This mission to the church and world should bring hope, health and wholeness through Christ. It should bear witness to and exemplify the saving, renewing, transforming grace of Jesus Christ. Mission should empower people to health and wholeness by helping to see themselves as positive agents of self and of global transformation. Mission means feeding, helping, and enabling people to experience justice, peace, wellness, and vitality on all levels of life. It means giving people spiritual and physical food—food to feed their bodies as well as their souls.

SUMMARY

Mission means not simply giving people something to eat but teaching them how to develop the confidence, and internal and external resources that will enable them to feed themselves and others. This care and feeding begins with the soul of the individual and translates to the body as well as to the larger community and world. By being in mission to themselves, community, and world, mainline denominations can establish a new presence in the world and receive a fresh outpouring of God's spirit of revitalization for a bright and glorious future as they give witness to the continuing reign of Christ.

10

Reclaiming the Value of the Church for Ministry

See the Gospel Church secure, And founded on a Rock! All her promises are sure; Her bulwarks who can shock?

—*Charles Wesley*

We should reclaim the value of the church for ministry in these times. The church should not be a place where everyone automatically lowers their standard, or gives half-baked service because it is the church. The church should be a place where standards are raised, expectations are high, and the ministry is valued. People give their best to the world, but then give less than their best to the church. Regrettably, they do not understand that their blessings come from God and nothing pleases God more than when people value God's work, mission, ministry, and church. We cannot call ourselves followers of Christ and have great expectations of Christ and low expectations of ourselves. We are sinners, yes, but the grace and mercy of God gives us new opportunities for renewal and service.

"I Don't Feel No Ways Tired"

If everything that you do in ministry is results oriented and you don't get the results you expect you either stop pressing altogether and forget about it, or you press harder until you achieve your goals and objectives. Each of us wants to get to a point in our service where we can say continuously the words of that old great hymn, "I don't feel no ways tired." In other words, no matter what I personally experience in service, I will press on with joy and enthusiasm because success is measured not so much by the results I obtain but by the faith I keep in doing God's work.

It is true that we live in a real world and we expect to see the fruits of our labors realized. We want our church to grow, souls to be saved, new members to join, and spiritual support provided that will culminate in the positive transformation of people's lives for Christ. We want our churches to be creative, positive environments where people can realize their spiritual gifts, grow in Christ, and excel in kingdom building.

We all know people who have served their congregations for many years who have sustained their enthusiasm through the highs and lows of ministry. They have never lost their energy for service. They have a wisdom and understanding about people and the ministry. They know how to pace themselves. They have a servant's heart, an undying and unyielding passion and love for service.

How do these leaders sustain their energy for ministry and the church? They do it by leading a strong prayer life, keeping a sense of humor by laughing at themselves and with others, and by spending time with their families. In addition, they often set small goals and work assiduously toward achieving those goals. Too often our goals are too large, too unrealistic, and we set the conditions for defeat before we get started. Too many defeats can lead to dispassion, despair, and ultimately, inertia. I was advised early on in my ministry to start small and work small. Achieving success in the little things would one day lead to bigger things. If things don't work out, always use the Lombardi philosophy of going back to basics. If you can execute the basics, you can enjoy some measure of success that will fuel your passion to be more and do more for Christ.

I remember a famous scene in the movie *Lawrence of Arabia*. Lawrence is standing before an army officer holding a lighter under his hand and the flame is burning his palm. He holds the flame there for a long period of time and never screams in pain. When asked by the officer how he was able to achieve this feat without even a grimace, Lawrence replied, "You have to not mind it hurting."

Sometimes we have to develop a mind-set that does not worry when things go awry in our service. After all, we are imperfect people, living in an imperfect world, and things are bound to go askew. When we understand that people are capable of great things and mundane things, that we are all sinners saved by grace, we can develop an understanding, compassion, or patience that forgives the weaknesses of others. As leaders, we must at times leave room for insanity so that we don't lose our minds and spirit for service. We must not mind people making mistakes. We must not kill our wounded in our kingdom building.

We must remember that the freedom to fail prepares people for the opportunity to succeed. We must keep failure and human frailty in perspective. The truth is, ministry is not for chumps or the fainthearted. As leaders we must be prepared to hold our ground, go to the cross, and suffer redemptively for the sake of the growth and empowerment of God's people.

RECLAIMING GOD'S CHURCH

If we are to reclaim God's church we must have holy boldness and not be afraid to retrieve key elements of our tradition. We must not be afraid to return to the basics to build ourselves up for the glory of God. Everything we do must be done so that the Lord will be magnified, the Son will be glorified, the Holy Ghost will be verified, believers will be edified, and the devil will be horrified. The church should be a:

- preservation center of the gospel

- transformation center for lost souls, God's people, and the community

- healing center for the broken, discouraged, and those who need to repent and be forgiven

- hospitality center for the lost and lonely

- prayer, praise, and worship center for Christ

- an educational center to teach Christian values and principles and how to fight the good fight

- community center for the milieu it is called to serve

- spiritual, relational, familial, vocational, social, political, and economic empowerment center for the people and community

- center for the proclamation of God's truth

More than any other thing, the church should be a spiritual empowerment center for the people of God and community; and spiritual empowerment and growth are the infrastructures for numerical growth. We cannot talk of numerical growth and empowerment without first dealing with spiritual growth and empowerment among members and constituents. Not every church will grow into a mega-membership. However, every church can experience spiritual growth, the foundation to all church growth God's way.

A MODEL: THE WESLEYAN EVANGELICAL PARADIGM OF MINISTRY

Effective ministry is not only true to the precepts of denomination but the precepts of culture and context. Any serious leadership reconfiguration in mainline denominations, such as United Methodism, must seriously examine evangelical paradigms for ministry. We must find ways to establish dialogue between text and context, denomination, and community. Configuring new models of leadership requires ongoing dialogue between these various poles of human, cultural, and institutional concern.

John Wesley, the founder of Methodism, established a very effective model of ministry that viewed the texts and contexts of ministry as vitally important. His central struggle with the Church of England was its negation of context as a feasible starting place to minister the gospel to the people of God. Social and economic station need not be the sole criteria for valuing the worth of recipients of the ministry. The precocity of Wesley's model is based on several assumptions which can be appropriated as we minister in our various communities. We can retrieve successful principles of the past and apply them to our current contexts for future success.

The first of the most important aspects of Wesley's ministry was that it was highly *biblical*. The Word of God was a central focus of his ministry and the example of Jesus was a principal catalyst in Wesley's ministerial formation. Successful models of ministry must be *Word centered* and *Word oriented*. The problem with biblical illiteracy in the larger culture is not that people *can't* read the Word of God. The problem with biblical illiteracy in the church is that people *won't* read the Word of God.

Successful and innovative leadership models must seriously consider the role of the Word in the spiritual formation of leaders and laity in the church and in the profiles of ministry of the church in community. Wesley understood the power and value of Scripture in shaping models of ministry, in cultivating spiritual consciousness, and in empowering people to realize gifts, graces, and potential amid indigent circumstances. The power of the Word for Wesley then, and for pastors now, resides in its capacity to move the people of God from disabilities to possibilities and into empowerment thinking and conscious action which will bring persons to Christ and transform the world.

Affirming that Wesley's ministry was highly biblical does not simply mean that the contemporary experiences of believers were historically retrofitted to make sense of the gospel, but that the Bible was utilized as a hermeneutic for shaping and influencing the current existential reality. Biblical modes of ministry not only faithfully retrieve scriptural texts as viable pretexts for the praxis of ministry, but also equally provide an existential framework out of which all contemporary life and existence can be meaningfully actualized and interpreted. Thus the power of Wesley's model was that the Bible was not simply a tool for evangelization of those who needed Christ, but also provided a living framework, a context in which they could discover new meanings and nuances of empowerment that made a qualitative difference in their lives as lived in the here and now.

The second important aspect of Wesley's ministry is that it was highly *evangelical*. A certain fervor and spiritual zeal punctuated and enveloped Wesley's missional efforts which invariably compelled him onward and outward to reach the plain people of England. Being evangelical meant that he never had a wait-and-see approach to ministry, except in those matters where he was attending to answers and directions from God.

To evangelize is to go out beyond the confines of the community, church, and environment to win persons to Christ. In this respect, Wesley was very aggressive and highly entrepreneurial in seeking and sharing Christ. Because Christ went out, Wesley went out to preach and teach the gospel. His method of evangelization was successful because it conveyed to the people that the church needed them and they needed Christ.

Present-day churches should "go out" rather than sit still waiting to see who will come to them. A nurturing and entrepreneurial spirit must be established, where people, confident in the Word, are unafraid to move beyond the four walls of the church with zeal and enthusiasm for the gospel. Had Wesley not gone out into the highways and byways of England, Methodism would likely not exist.

Part of the success formula of contemporary ministry is to assert oneself for Christ, to aggressively hit the streets, and to compel persons to Christ. Standing still in our comfort zones and spiritual safe houses will not bring persons into the fold of the fellowship of believers. Churches must seek the lost and let people know that they need the church and the church needs them.

The third important feature of Wesley's ministry was *cultural*. When all is said and done, winning people to Jesus requires some measure of cultural fluency and Wesley's success was predicated on his knowledge in relating to people in terms and in language they could fully fathom. Reaching the plain people of England meant he spoke to them in plain terms so they could derive plain understanding that would urge them to plain action for Christ. Wesley knew that culture was highly important. He knew how to speak in the colors and nuances of plain English culture so that the people were moved to tears, action, confession, or repentance on behalf of Christ.

Effective church leadership must be culturally relevant. Church leaders must familiarize themselves with the cultural assumptions and landscape of the communities they serve. For example, it makes no sense for black churches in black communities which are emotionally and spiritually teeming with rhythm, life, laughter, and rhyme, to develop worship styles and ministries that are dead, dull, and sad. If the community pulsates with life and vitality, the center of that community, the church, should be the epitome of spiritual and cultural enthusiasm. A dead church in an alive community makes strange helpmates. African American churches in African American communities should demonstrate cultural fluency and appreciation for African American culture. Pastors and laity must be comfortable walking the talk of the African American people. They should have a sense for the diversity and varieties of culture within their own communities and develop viable ministries based on cultural needs. Cultural fluency is the passport into the people's minds and hearts and an integral part of the success of any viable congregation.

Wesley understood that deculturalization of a people leads inherently to their devaluation as a people and that's why he used the gospel to bridge the cultural gaps between diverse segments of the community as well as used it as a means of unifying the threads of cultural empowerment of the plain people of England.

A fourth hallmark of Wesley's ministry is that it was also highly *prophetic*. Here the emphasis is on the gospel as a source of personal and social transformation. He realized that you could not empower people with the Word of God without equipping them with the knowledge and courage to transform their existing social condition. The focus here is on transformation of both self and community. For Wesley, the gospel was a spiritual and social force for positive transformation which laid the solid foundation of biblical and social witness for Christ inherent in early Methodism.

The transformation and melioration of existing conditions is an important part of the church's mission and ministry. Providing people with the knowledge and facility for human and social transformation is one of the church's greatest benchmarks.

Finally, a fifth aspect of the Wesleyan paradigm of ministry was *spiritual*. Here the focus is on those transcendent aspects of the gospel and its ministry that prepare people for the disciplined practice of the spiritual life. A gift of spirituality as a vocation in the Wesleyan perspective is the cultivation of discipline through devotion, prayer, Bible study, fasting, and other methods of spiritual enhancement. Translating spiritual concepts into precepts is part of the missional charge of the church and its ministries. Cultivating the discipline of spirituality was a central focus of Wesley's ministry and was later translated into church polity and structures which relied heavily upon a disciplined clergy and laity for organization and survival. Methodism could not have survived without the avid workings of the Holy Spirit and the spiritual discipline of clergy and laity. By retrieving, analyzing, and implementing ministries which are highly *biblical, evangelical, cultural, prophetic,* and *spiritual,* mainline denominations can adopt Wesley's blueprint of successful principles as a foundation for a viable future.

Mainline churches can again become vital places of power, energy, and joy, but they must reprioritize the importance of spiritual transformation and praxis. Churches can become vital again by daring like their predecessors to become radically Christlike. They must have the courage to take a long hard look at themselves and to admit where change is needed.

In order for the mainline churches to be changed, the people in the church need to change their thinking, orientation, and the assumptions about the way they do ministry. They must step outside of hegemonic, hierarchical thinking and have the courage to trust Christ enough to be transformed. They must also discard homogenized thinking that says only our way of doing things is the best way. This is certainly thinking that engenders suicide on the installment plan. Too many people in too many places of church authority have the attitude of omniscience. Rather than admitting they do not know and seeking help, they, like pharaoh, become more arrogant and hard-hearted and pride goes before the fall.

We cannot become a spiritually vital church by leaving God out of our proceedings. We must seek the transformative presence and power of the Holy Spirit. We must fast and pray and seek God's will for our lives. Mainline denominations should have calls to renewal and revitalization within their ranks and within the world. They must shirk the image of a silent church in the wake of continuing racism, sexism, and the devastations of globalization. The church should speak to the continuing corruptions of our society where petty thieves are given long prison sentences while corporate raiders who steal billions are never indicted. The church has obviated itself by turning a deaf ear to the continuing crimes and corruptions in our midst. But how can the church have the power and strength to sustain a concern for such issues when it has undermined or discarded its greatest power source, its own spirituality?

How can mainline churches truly reenergize and revitalize themselves except through Christ and the anointive, transformative grace of the Holy Spirit? We cannot put our spirituality on the back burner simply to fit in with the world or because we feel that spirituality is no longer in style and expect to have genuine transformative power. We kill ourselves when we leave God and the Holy Spirit out of our thinking and our doing for Christ. We must go back to the basics. We must retrieve a foundational spirituality that practices grace, repentance, and forgiveness, a spirituality that prophetically calls both the church and the world into account.

SUMMARY

We reclaim the value of the church for ministry when we reclaim Christ, God, and the Holy Spirit, when we reclaim those incentives and dynamics that make us life-giving, life-fulfilling movements when we started out.

None of the mainline churches started out dead because they had the power of the Holy Ghost blessing, guiding, and anointing their pastors and laypeople. Wesley, Luther, Edwards, and others were all under the influence of the Holy Ghost. They used their bodies, minds, and souls to glorify God. They were not corrupted by the status quo, nor permanent slaves to previous traditions; they boldly broke rank and did something new, as did Christ.

We need that same spirit today: a spirit of openness and adventure; a fresh spirit of renewal, energy, and vitality; a spirit that does not cower to evil nor shun critical sustained self-evaluation and analysis. We need a spirit of justice, truth, mercy, and grace. If we don't claim it and use it, we will be like the movements we originally broke from and become staid, stagnant, stifling, lifeless forces who have sold our birthright to evil and the mediocrity of this world. To reclaim spiritual vitality, we must reclaim Christ so that wholeness and wellness can be our mission and mantra for a glorious future. Warren Wiersbe puts it plainly: "When the church trying to reach the world became like the world, she lost her impact on the world. How tragic that we cooperated with the enemy in breaking down our own walls. We lost our distinctiveness and destroyed our own defenses" (*Be Quoted*. Grand Rapids: Baker Books, 2000, 38).

11

RECLAIMING THE IMPORTANCE OF THE BLACK CHURCH

The only place blacks felt they could maintain an element of self-expression was the church.

—Richard Allen

Since the genesis of many mainline denominations, black people have played a decisive role in their development. Virtually all mainline denominations have black congregations and many black people have made significant contributions to those denominations.

Unfortunately, as mainline denominations have declined, so too has the presence of many viable black congregations. In the Detroit Conference of The United Methodist Church alone, the number of black congregations has dwindled decisively. The spiritual malaise that has infected the larger church has also imperiled the African American church within mainline denominations.

Part of the decline of black churches has been due to the fact that in an effort to assimilate into the larger white denominations, many black churches have lost the spiritual fervor and fire of black old-time religion that has traditionally appealed to the African American masses. Rather than retain the authenticity and uniqueness of black religion, many of those churches have forsaken the more vital aspects of black spirituality in order to be accepted by their white counterparts. Instead of developing churches spiritually on fire for Christ that coalesce the authentic remnants of black spirituality with the vital elements of the larger denomination, many black churches have disassociated themselves from the religion of black folk entirely, precipitating in part the churches' decline.

The current malaise and atrophy affecting mainline churches has also spilled over into African American churches. An identity crisis now plagues black churches where many are torn between whether to be denominationally "correct" by imitating the larger white church or to be spiritually "correct" and true to the grain of their own wood. Imitation, the sincerest form of flattery, may be the worst practice, especially when what we are imitating is not nearly as vital as what we already have.

Spiritual vitality is not exclusive to white or black culture. Both black and white churches can possess spiritual vitality and be on fire for Christ. The problem is that churches and cultures abandon those principles and practices that have worked for them over the years in order to become accepted by other cultures or people who practice religion differently. **We must reclaim the importance of the black church.**

Why should the black church relinquish its rich history of spirituality in order to identify with churches that are spiritually dull, lifeless, and even lethargic? Why should the black church commit spiritual suicide by mimicking principles and practices of the religion of other folk just to make those other folk feel good? Why should the black church develop models of religion and spirituality that have not worked for the souls of black folk since their sojourn here in America?

The greatest sin is to not be true to who and what one is

authentically. So rather than develop a religion and church life that is spiritually vital and alive, numerous black churches have adopted the traditions of other folk to their own detriment.

The black church has always been a vital force in American life. Without the black church and black religion, black people may not have come this far in their struggle for sanity, humanity, and wholeness. Without belief in God, African Americans would have perished in the doldrums of slavery and in the grip of Jim Crow.

What are some of the traditions of the black church that have been so vital over the years? The traditions and culture of expressive spirituality, the power of call and response, worship traditions that are energetic, alive, and wholesome. Equally important is the role of the black preacher as the chief shepherd and primary spiritual authority in the church. The role of the black pastor in the black church is a powerful role. In an effort to imitate the culture and tradition of some other churches, black churches have subordinated the role of the black minister in shaping the ethos and trajectory of black church life. In some churches, black pastors have absolutely no spiritual authority. They function more like puppets than they do as spiritual leaders and so long as congregations hold their spiritual leaders to this role those churches will never succeed God's way. They will never find the growth, power, and vitality they need to overcome their present sickness.

Collaborative models of ministry do work well in black churches. This in no way means to obviate the role of laity in shaping the direction and destiny of black congregations. Healthy churches develop partnerships or covenants between pastors and laity. However, I am referring to the general culture of contempt that permeates black churches that often trickles down from the way mainline churches view pastors and pastoral authority. The pastor in many of those churches is not a true spiritual leader or religious servant of the Lord, but a peon functionary who takes orders from a laity who don't know the Word of God nor are under the influence of the Holy Ghost!

Too many would-be strong pastoral leaders have their spiritual power and authority eclipsed or domesticated by people who are not spiritually grounded. In an effort to please everybody and to get along with folk in the "big house," they throw away their pastoral authority because they are afraid to stand up and suffer and to be counted in the fight. What black leaders don't realize is that folk in the big house don't want them to throw away their leadership abilities just to fit in with the people who are called to lead.

If mainline churches are to reclaim the power of the black church, they must understand the prominent role the black pastor plays in shaping the health and life of black churches. To be a servant leader, if we are to use this model, does not mean to be a weak leader, a manipulated leader, a spineless leader who has not the courage to lead the church he or she has been appointed to serve.

In black and white churches, pastors have a vital and powerful role in shaping the life of those churches. Without strong pastors in any denomination, churches will not move, grow, and thrive in ways that give glory to God. Without strong black pastors, mainline churches will have few strong black congregations.

The way mainline churches view the practice of ministry, the nature and temperament of those called to ministry and the culture, and the traditions and ethos of local congregations all influence the tone and destiny of the black church. The black church is not only a spiritual life center but a life center in African American communities. To mimic the tired and listless practices of some denominations will never appeal to the sensibilities and needs of the black masses. No one wants to be a part of anything tired or dead. The practice of religion and spirituality should raise expectations and excitement about what the living God can do rather than lower or dash those expectations. When religion is practiced in tired, monolithic, lifeless ways, no one—black or white—wants to be a part. Our enthusiasm for Christ raises expectations about the power and possibilities of God; it creates within people a hopeful expectancy that God truly lives and reigns in our time.

White mainline churches should have the courage to examine the way some black folk do church. Why should African Americans always view themselves through the windows of other races and cultures? Why can't other races and cultures view themselves through the windows and prisms of African Americana? Our experience as a people is as vital and valid as any other culture, race, or ethnic group. Why then are we encouraged to view ourselves through other people's eyes and windows to receive validation and legitimacy? Why can't others view themselves through our lenses and also find validation as children of God? African Americans have much to teach this world about the practice of spirituality, about how to survive under holocaust conditions. Why shouldn't other people look to the black church and the example we have given them of what it means to be spiritual so they might understand how to become spiritually strong in a crazy world?

If mainline churches want to reclaim spiritual vitality, they should have the courage to study and evaluate how the black church has survived over the centuries; how an adaptive and expressive spirituality has given new meaning and power to the souls of black folk. Unfortunately, many of those denominations can't look to many black churches within their fold for positive examples of this because too many black churches have imitated the larger church and are dying the same slow, agonizing death as their mother churches.

To reclaim the black church, black congregations must also realize that white denominations are not going to save them. Black folk must develop a mind-set for saving themselves. A culture of codependency permeates many black congregations in the expectation that "white folk will take care of us." This culture of expectancy and codependency is warranted in some instances. The larger church should be committed to saving and nurturing struggling black churches. However, when a culture of dependency is cultivated and a climate of ingenuity, self-sufficiency, and independence are not fostered, perpetual dependency is created which cripples and ultimately kills black churches. At times, black congregations adopt the mind-set that, as long as other folk are taking care of me, I don't have to develop the resources to care for myself. Some support should be given but after a while the local church should be on its own. Those churches should take in new members and develop the resources to pay and support pastors and staff. If a church is not taking in new members, it cannot develop the membership base to financially and spiritually support the local church unless it has other resources. If it does not have the financial wherewithal to take care of itself, and transformations within the culture of that church to make it more sufficient do not occur, the question is *how long can it survive in a state of codependency?*

The exception to this of course is mission outreach churches which need continual support from the mother church to minister to the needs of the economically poor and indigent. Denominations have a responsibility for taking care of such churches.

But what about those churches that are in viable communities that still have not grown and become self-sufficient? What are the causes of such stagnation? Is it inept pastors who have no energy, charisma, or passion for ministry and are instead simply branch managers overseeing the obsolescence of increasing irrelevant and lifeless churches? Is it tired preaching and worship services? Is it intractable congregations who do not want to grow or change, congregations who run new people away and suffocate the Holy Spirit out of the life of their churches because they are more interested in fixing, managing, and controlling the life of the church than in enabling it to grow? Is it a culture of codependency which has undercut and diminished the creativity and industry of local congregations? Is it the way denominations have traditionally done ministry in accordance with white middle-class, enlightenment values, and their refusal to adopt new ideas and models that have killed churches? There is an old adage that says "Never trust a doctor whose office plants have died." Can this axiom be applied to denominations whose church death rate is greater than their growth rate?

Reclaiming the black church means more than developing Band-Aid®, fast money fixes to alleviate rather than eradicate the seeds of decline. The problem is the current culture of denominations who refuse to change because they are encumbered by the bureaucracies they serve and they do not allow the Holy Spirit to lead and guide them out of their problems. The problem is the culture of church in a post-Christian era who has lost what it means to model vital Christian spirituality.

When the black church, which has managed to maintain spiritual viability throughout centuries of racism and oppression, begins to die, then those mainline churches really are in trouble. If the black church in mainline denominations which has managed to survive through hell and high water is dying, what must it do to save itself? Herbert Marcuse said that the great genius of American culture has been its capacity to assimilate its opposition. In the assimilation of the black church into the larger denominations, has it lost some of its spiritual fervor and fire?

It is my belief that the black church and black spirituality will and has played a vital role in saving America. If the black church in mainline Protestant denominations dies, what does this say about the church itself and the denominations of which it has been traditionally an integral and viable part? The question then is not only what the denominations will do to revitalize and save black churches, but also what will those churches do to save themselves? This is the question of our time as black churches continue to die at almost epidemic rates and to go on "mission support" in mainline denominations.

Mainline churches must do more than have the same old people work on the same old problems. Many of those people are part of the problem. Mainline churches must have the courage like General Motors and Taco Bell to talk to the consumer or would-be church-goer to discover what they are looking for in a church. All the answers will not come from people currently within the system because their thinking has been conditioned. They have adopted a certain linear mindset that thinks about problems and solutions along the same old trajectories. That's why they keep getting the same old results.

Talk to the man or woman on the street. Talk to people who are growing expanding churches and not just theoreticians who develop models willy-nilly and expect them to apply in every situation. Talk to the unchurched person to find out why he or she rarely attends a mainline church. Talk to God and to the Holy Spirit and ask for directions rather than assuming that you already have all the answers. Don't be afraid to admit that you don't have all the answers and that you need help. Such help may come from nontraditional sources. If you want to know anything about the nature and ethos of an organization, talk to the janitor or nonadministrative people. Talk to the people on the fringes, the virtually marginalized folk who are not customarily thought to be in the know. By reclaiming the power and importance of the black church, mainline denominations will reclaim a vital portion of its answer to its future vitality and success.

SUMMARY

Reclaiming the black church is key to spiritual revitalization in mainline churches. Black religion and black spirituality have been important resources in creating and meaningfully sustaining the African American experience. The black church has much to teach the larger culture about survival and the practice of spirituality under adverse conditions. If mainline churches continue to lose the presence and legacy of African American churches, it will continue to lose its appeal to the broader masses. The black church has traditionally been a vital church. Those elements of black church tradition that have made it vital and resourceful should be retained as a basis for building churches in the future.

Appendix A: Suggestions for Reclaiming Spiritual Vitality

Mainline Churches Should Reclaim:

1. The presence and power of the Holy Spirit to lead, anoint, and empower the churches' ministry.

2. The importance of conversion experience and being born again for each believer and denominational official and for the renewal of denominational structures.

3. The value and priority of saving souls at the denominational and local church levels.

4. Expressive, transformative, and celebrative worship services.

5. Expressive, transformative, and servant-oriented service in ministry.

6. The Bible as the undergirding authority for ministry.

7. The purpose, meaning, and lifestyle of holiness.

8. The value and employment of all spiritual gifts for service in the church and the world.

9. Passionate and spirit-filled preaching.

10. A heritage of evangelical fervor, fire, and social commitment that leads to social justice and the practice of peace.

11. Foundational principles or back to basics classes for membership, discipleship, worship, stewardship, and fellowship.

12. Nontraditional thinking that compels denominational officials to think outside of the box and to employ new strategies for operating denominational structures and entities under the influence of the Holy Spirit.

13. Priorities that challenge denominations to transform cumbersome and burdensome denominational organizations into life-giving, soul-saving organizations.

14. Prophetic witness that eliminates the church's conspiracies of silence and brings truth to power.

15. Mission to local as well as global communities to eradicate poverty, hunger, and disease.

16. Cultural relevancy to and fluency in specific communities.

17. Denominational leaders who are not afraid of positive change for existing structures.

18. Church leaders who are open to spiritual formation and transformation by developing strong prayer and devotional lives of service.

19. The value of prayer, fasting, and other spiritual disciplines as a basis for spiritual growth and empowerment.

20. Developing a mission to transform internal denominational structures as well as outward social structures.

21. A vision for the future.

22. The importance of the black church.

APPENDIX B: QUESTIONS FOR RECLAIMING SPIRITUAL VITALITY

Does your church openly discuss the Holy Spirit and what it means to be transformed through Christ?

Does your church emphasize the importance of having a conversion experience or of being born again?

Does your church emphasize holiness and sanctification as a spiritually foundational lifestyle?

Does your church welcome, nurture, and practice all spiritual gifts?

Has your church reclaimed the evangelical aspects of its heritage as a basis for present empowerment and growth?

Does your church stress the importance of spiritual disciplines and spiritual praxis for its leaders and members?

Does your church train its leaders spiritually for leadership in the local church?

Does your church have a vision for the next three to five years?

Does your denomination spiritually empower its members to save souls and to become effective disciples for Christ?

Do denominational leaders conduct Bible studies and stress the value of personal spiritual formation as a means of growing in Christ?

Do bishops and other church leaders take an active role in the spiritual care of clergy and laity?

Does your denomination emphasize the importance of passionate preaching for soul winning and church building?

What is the state of the black church in your denomination?

What is the nature of missions in your church?

Do you have mission programs that minister to the needs of parishioners and the larger community?

Do you have mission programs that address the concerns of social justice in local communities?

In what ways is your denomination developing viable ways of transforming itself for the future?

BIBLIOGRAPHY

Anderson, Leith. *Dying for Change*. Minneapolis: Bethany House, 1990.

Bandy, Thomas G. *Kicking Habits: Welcome Relief for Addicted Churches*. Nashville: Abingdon Press, 2001.

Beard, Steve, et al. *Power, Holiness, and Evangelism: Rediscovering God's Purity, Power, and Passion for the Lost*. Compiled by Randy Clark. Shippensburg, Pa.: Destiny Image Publishers, 1999.

Berkley, James D., ed. *Leadership Handbook of Outreach and Care*. Grand Rapids: Baker Books, 2001.

———. *Leadership Handbook on Preaching and Worship*. Grand Rapids: Baker Books, 2000.

———. *Leadership Handbook on Administration*. Grand Rapids: Baker Books, 2000.

Bruggemann, Walter. *Biblical Perspectives on Evangelism: Living in a Three-storied Universe*. Nashville: Abingdon Press, 1993.

Buchan, Jim. *Apostolic Evangelism: Can You Hear the Call?* Mansfield, Pa.: Fire Wind, 2001.

Buttry, Daniel. *Bringing Your Church Back to Life: Beyond Survival Mentality*. Valley Forge, Pa.: Judson Press, 1988.

Carothers, J. Edward. *The Paralysis of Mainstream Protestant Leadership.* Nashville: Abingdon Press, 1990.

Claerbaut, David. *Urban Ministry.* Grand Rapids: Zondervan Pub. House, 1983.

Coleman, Robert E. *The Master Plan of Evangelism.* Grand Rapids: F. H. Revell, 1993.

————. *The Master's Way of Personal Evangelism.* Wheaton, Ill.: Crossway Books, 1997.

Cueni, Robert. *The Vital Church Leader.* Nashville: Abingdon Press, 1991.

Dunagin, Richard L. with Lyle E. Schaller. *Beyond These Walls: Building the Church in a Built-out Neighborhood.* Nashville: Abingdon Press, 1999.

Easum, William. *How to Reach Baby Boomers.* Nashville: Abingdon Press, 1991.

Harper, Nile. *Urban Churches, Vital Signs: Beyond Charity Toward Justice.* Grand Rapids: W. B. Eerdmans Pub., 1999.

Hendrichsen, Walter A. *Disciples Are Made—Not Born: How to Help Others Grow to Maturity in Christ.* Wheaton, Ill.: Victor Books, 2002.

Hunter, George G., III *Leading and Managing a Growing Church.* Nashville: Abingdon Press, 2000.

Jones, Ezra Earl. *Strategies for New Churches.* New York: Harper & Row, 1976.

June, Lee N., and Matthew Parker, eds. *Evangelism and Discipleship in African-American Churches.* Grand Rapids: Zondervan Pub. House, 1999.

Liardon, Roberts. *Breaking Controlling Powers.* Tulsa, Okla.: Albury Pub., 2000.

Malone, Tom. *Essentials of Evangelism.* Grand Rapids: Kregel, 1958.

McGarran, Donald and George G. Hunter, III *Church Growth Strategies That Work.* Nashville: Abingdon Press, 1980.

McNeal, Reggie. *Revolution in Leadership: Training Apostles for Tomorrow's Church.* Nashville: Abingdon Press, 1998.

Meeks, Wayne A. *The First Urban Christians: The Social World of the Apostle Paul.* New Haven: Yale University Press, 1983.

Neuenschwander, Mark and Betty Neuenschwander. *Crisis Evangelism.* Ventura, Calif.: Regal, 1999.

Parsons, George and Speed B. Leas. *Understanding Your Congregation as a System: The Manual.* Bethesda, Md.: Alban Institute, 1993.

Sande, Ken. *The Peacemaker: A Biblical Guide to Solving Personal Conflict.* Grand Rapids: Baker Books, 1997.

Schaller, Lyle E. *Effective Church Planning.* Nashville, Abingdon Press, 1979.

———. *Growing Plans.* Nashville: Abingdon Press, 1983.

Stewart, Carlyle F., III. *Street Corner Theology: Indigenous Reflections on the Reality of God in the African-American Experience.* Nashville: J. C. Winston Pub., 1996.

———. *The Empowerment Church: Speaking a New Language for Church Growth.* Nashville: Abingdon Press, 2001.

———. *Black Spirituality and Black Consciousness: Soul Force, Culture, and Freedom in African-American Experience.* Trenton, N.J.: Africa World Press, 1999.

———. *Soul Survivors: An African American Spirituality.* Louisville: John Knox Press, 1997.

Villafañe, Eldin, et al. *Transforming the City: Reframing Education for Urban Ministry.* Grand Rapids: W. B. Eerdmans, 2002.

Wiersbe, Warren. *Be Quoted: from A to Z with Warren W. Wiersbe.* Edited by James R. Adair. Grand Rapids, Mich.: Baker Books, 2000.